THE FINNISH MIRACLE

To Steve Wuori,

I hope you enjoy these stories about Finland.

Regards,

[signature]

Helsinki, 15.10.2013

ANDRÉ NOËL CHAKER

THE FINNISH MIRAGE MIRACLE

An inspiring model and
a few cool stories from a self-made nation

Talentum, Helsinki 2011

To my Finnish family,
my three inspiring Finnish miracles.

Contents

Introduction 9
The miracle of Finland 9
The Possibility Model 13

CHAPTER 1: An open mind 19
1.1 The first step 19
1.2 The ruthless egalitarian 27
1.3 Education, education and education 43
1.4 Still room for a stretch 51

CHAPTER 2: Trial and error 63
2.1 The hierarchy of trial and error 64
2.2 Olympic trials and tribulations 87

CHAPTER 3: Working harder and smarter 105
3.1 A working formula 107
3.2 The Finnish cult of work 113
3.3 A wealth of wits 119
3.4 A culture of trust and well-being 131
3.5 Working the Nokia way 144
3.6 Things to work on 151

CHAPTER 4: Sisu — 159

4.1 *Sisu* and success — 159
4.2 *Sisu* at war — 162
4.3 *Sisu* in business — 175
4.4 *Sisu* in sports — 177
4.5 The bad *sisu* — 181

CHAPTER 5: Being yourself — 199

5.1 Getting personal — 205
5.2 Authenticity — 221
5.3 In ourselves we trust — 235

The miracle of you — 249

Acknowledgements — 253
Appendix 1 — 255
Notes — 257
Index — 265

Introduction

Be realistic: Plan for a miracle.
Osho Rajneesh

The miracle of Finland

I have always been interested in what makes people, businesses and nations succeed. Our eternal quest for success at all levels of our lives is an intrinsic part of the human condition. It is the motor that keeps most of us moving forward from one day to the next.

Success, of course, means different things to different people. It also has frames of reference that vary greatly on the basis of national culture. For the purposes of this book, I have given success a plain and straightforward definition. It is the fulfillment of a set of personal or collective objectives. The cultural context for the success I speak of here is generally based on Western precepts and values, with a particular reference to the culture of Finland.

I am a Canadian immigrant turned into a *New Finn*. With over twenty years of my life spent in Finland, I will have soon spent more time in my adoptive country than in my native Canada. For most of my career I have worked in international organizations and businesses. I have had the pleasure and privilege of working closely with people representing dozens of different cultures and language groups from all over the world.

When I discovered Finland and its special culture, I was immediately impressed with the country and its spirit. I have come to believe that there is something special about *Finnishness* to the point where I ultimately felt the need to produce a book like this.

Finnishness is here defined as a set of cultural and behavioral characteristics shared by most people living in Finland. In these pages, I present a general roadmap for success called the *Possibility Model*. It is presented in the form of a mountain climb marked by several determining stops on the ascent to possible success. For each one of these stops, I use Finnish examples, stories and testimonials of success and failure. Through this exercise, I hope the reader will gain a new perspective on generating successes at all levels, as well as an original outlook on Finland and its people.

In the minds of some, Finland is a miracle. Not in its size or in its impact on world affairs, but in its survival against the odds and in the way that it currently thrives. The Finnish state is near the top of the world both geographically and in terms of a wide range of social and economic measures. Indeed, during their short national history, the Finns have been doing a lot of things right. In Finland, I have seen miracles happen, large and small, and many of them are presented here on paper for the benefit of those who may find them inspiring.

In its evolution as a nation, Finland can be considered a success under many of the most common and significant international standards. Some recent international benchmarks include:

- The best country in the world; *Newsweek Magazine* 2010

- Best basic education in the world; *PISA* 2003, 2006

- Happiest country in the world (along with Denmark); *Gallup World Poll* 2010

- Least corrupt country in the world; *Transparency International* 2007 (always in the top 10 since then)

- Top ten most-competitive country in the world; World *Economic Forum* 2000-2011

These represent an enviable record for a young nation that has come a long way in gaining its independence and developing its prosperity. Indeed, at the end of the 19th century, Finns were beleaguered by famine and poverty. In the early 20th century the country fell into a highly divisive civil war. During World War II, Finland fought an incredible set of wars against both the mighty Soviet Union and Nazi Germany. In the mid-20th century the country had to build an industrial base practically from scratch to pay its war debts. These highlights from Finland's historical trials are certainly evidence that what doesn't kill you makes you stronger. It also puts the list of stellar national accomplishments listed above and those coming later in this book into better perspective.

Like many nations, however, Finland has faced and still faces challenges: it is by no means a perfect Shangri-La. In fact, when reading about their scores on some of the international studies mentioned above, many Finns remain skeptical and sometimes ask: "Are the other nations so bad?"

Indeed, studies such as the ones listed here are notoriously subjective and inexact by nature. Even for those at the top of these charts, there is still much room for improvement. In the end, we are all human, and humanity still has a long way to go before we can stop wishing for things to get better.

I have had the privilege of interviewing prominent Finnish persons from all walks of life in my quest for a better understanding of the relationship between Finnishness and success. The list of these Finns is reproduced in **Appendix 1** of this book. I am infinitely grateful to them for their time and for their special insights. With each of them, I initially asked four basic questions:

1. What is the greatest Finnish success story?

2. What is the greatest Finnish failure?

3. What trait of the Finnish character is the most conducive to success?

4. What trait of the Finnish character is the least conducive to success?

The answers they gave me were invaluable in adjusting the structure of this book and enriching its content. I do not reproduce all of their answers directly in this manuscript. I do, however, often refer to their views and stories at the relevant stage in our ascent of the *Possibility Model.*

Most of my interviewees told me that a native Finn would never have written a book like this. Indeed, it is not in the national character to promote yourself in Finland. This, as we will see, is one of the strengths and perhaps also one of the weaknesses of Finnishness. Finns also dislike and even distrust those who analyze an issue and then end up only having positive things to say about it.

Fortunately for them, as a trained lawyer in the art of *audi alteram partem,* I also believe that our quest for the truth lies in our ability to argue both sides of an issue. For this reason, I have made it a point to include, at the end of each of the chapters of this book, the development opportunities that I see Finland would need to address in order to maintain its stellar social and economic record in the future.

Through its own chain of successes and failures, Finland has managed to pull off some spectacular successes. I call these "miracles." For the purposes of this book, a miracle is the manifestation of something so uncommon or unlikely that it stretches our belief of what is possible. The survival of Finland in its two wars against the Soviet Union and the creation of a dynamic modern economy, of which Nokia has been the global flagship, are two of the better-known Finnish miracles. There are, however, a host of other minor Finnish miracles that merit commentary and a look into the ways they were achieved.

The Possibility Model

For close to thirty years I have been an avid reader of literature that gives insight into how to create greater possibilities for myself and for others. In this regard, I became particularly attuned to business and social sciences literature. I have always wanted to create a comprehensive yet simple map of where people, companies and even countries are situated at a given stage of their development, with a view to improving our understanding of where they need to go. After failing to find a model to my liking, I decided to draft one of my own. This is how I stumbled onto the *Possibility Model.*

Most business and socio-economic models tend to focus on one part of the chain of actions we need to take in order to enhance our chances for success. Many focus on strategy and vision generation. Others are more hands-on and deliver insights into processes or organizational behavior and even cultural frameworks. Finally, there is a lot of self-help literature that attempts to enhance motivation and the importance of visualization of goals, with emotional appeals to being the best you can be.

Few books, however, have proposed a comprehensive view of how all these elements, and more, should come together in bringing the seemingly impossible into the realm of the possible. This book is an attempt at such a comprehensive approach. It is based on a generic model that allows you to better understand how to generate possibilities and thus improve your chances for success.

Most of us are inspired and fascinated by stories of the impossible made possible. These stories function as a driver of human development. The struggle to improve our lot or to achieve something that few of us have ever achieved is one of the motors of human progress. At the individual level, making the impossible possible is a notion that both humbles and inspires. For some, the impossible remains but a dream. For others it becomes a reality which sets a new benchmark for what others can hope to attain.

I believe that human miracles occur in part as a result of a certain state of mind, a certain way of living your life or conducting your business. I have summarized these elements in a framework called the *Possibility Model*, presented below in Figure I-1. This model includes five steps, a set of prerequisites for generating success. Each of these five steps provides the main topic for one of the five chapters of this book. The steps are as follows:

1. An open mind

2. Trial and error

3. Working harder AND smarter

4 *Sisu*

5. Being yourself

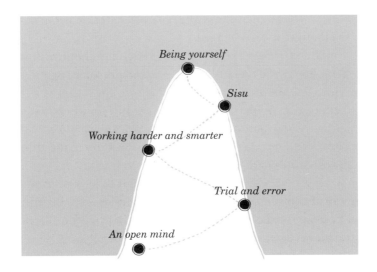

Figure I-1: **The Possibility Model**

These common catch phrases represent a process for making things happen. I have chosen them precisely because they are easy to remember and because they can, I think, significantly improve our lives if we simply take a fresh look at them in the Finnish context. When we put all five steps together, they form a powerful framework for understanding the workings of success. Their basic building blocks almost always form a solid part of the foundation of any human success story, whether personal or collective. Moreover, in the coverage of each stage of the *Possibility Model*, I have given these phrases a specific meaning as part of the larger story of success generation.

In Figure I-1, these five elements are metaphorically laid down as stages in a mountain climb. This could be any mountain, of course, but for the purposes of this book I have used a famous Finnish mountain: *Korvatunturi*. For non-Finnish readers this mountain may not ring a bell, but it has often played a role in making the seemingly impossible possible for millions of children across the world. This mountain is where Santa Claus and his elves do their perpetual work in preparation for Christmas.

Interestingly, the mountain's name in Finnish literally means "ear mountain," which suggests that Korvatunturi has the power to "listen" to the entire world and deliver on children's wishes everywhere. Such a place is quite fitting as a metaphor for the *Possibility Model* because of the mountain's mystical ability to connect to our youthful aspirations and help make our dreams come true.

The journey along the *Possibility Model* begins with keeping an open mind and ends with being oneself. These stages are set in order of difficulty. The assumption of the model is that it is more difficult to be yourself than to keep an open mind. The model also claims that it is far more challenging to face change and fear with something called Finnish *sisu* than to engage in trial and error.

Another assumption of this model is that each stage is a critical step that should occur in order to maximise your chances for success in any given venture. Though they may overlap to some extent, the earlier stages of the model form a solid sequential base on which the next stage can lay its own foundation.

Finally, the five steps identified here are by no means exhaustive of all the issues in the eternal quest for human success. They do, however, set forth what I believe to be one of the first comprehensive attempts to evaluate the most critical and sometimes contradictory elements in your journey towards success.

Inevitably, as we shall see in the Finnish stories from later chapters, several other issues come into play when we try to generate success. Pure luck, for example, is certainly one of them. The element of randomness in producing successes and even miracles is more specifically dealt with in Chapter 2, during our analysis of trial and error.

However, luck permeates our lives and our ventures from the beginning to the end. I believe that the forces of nature and chance and the forces of nurture and human action form a classic yin-and-yang, an essential synergetic dichotomy. You can't have one without the other, and both are inevitable contributors to the outcomes we achieve in life. If our impact on the direction of chance remains low, our ability to influence the nature and sequence of human action needed for success is much higher. This book focuses on the tangible human ability to influence success despite the shortcomings of random chance, which will always remain part of any winning equation.

It can also be said that success can come without systematically working through and succeeding at all of the stages of the model. It is indeed possible to move upward in the *Possibility Model* and achieve some level of success without having to master each and every one of the previous levels. Few persons and ventures actually perform a perfect ascent towards a successful outcome.

Still, even though you may not need to hit a perfect score at all five levels presented here, these stages are, for the majority of ventures, necessary steps in generating success. As performance improves at each level, the groundwork for making the impossible possible in your field becomes broader and stronger, and offers a greater catalyst for the human miracles you work for and hope to reach.

CHAPTER 1
An open mind

> Problems cannot be solved at the same
> level of awareness that created them.
>
> *Albert Einstein*

1.1 The first step

The foundation of success is an open mind. The rite of passage to the first level on the road to achievement takes place when we remove our barriers to what we perceive as being possible at a given time. The automatic uttering of "I don't know" or "that will never work" are the stumbling blocks over which many great ideas fall. Dismissive and self-defeating words, mechanically voiced at the suggestion of something new, often create a self-made and quite impenetrable iron barrier to potential innovations.

An initial negative reaction to the unknown is natural. The beaten path is all that one usually sees or hears about unless you actively keep an open mind. We are all faced with closed-mindedness, in others and in ourselves. Through fear or natural inclination, we believe much more easily in what is common, well-known and accepted. Yet while this may be the way many of us react to the unknown, it remains true that the mind is like a parachute: it produces better results when it is open.

This cumbersome feature of the human psyche is also present in the denial demonstrated when we are faced with the manifestation of unusual events. The consequences and scope of Acts of God or large-scale disasters are sometimes hard for people to accept or understand at the moment of their occurrence. For these people, it is only when a highly irregular event becomes widely publicized and discussed in the mainstream media that their minds begin to grasp the magnitude of what has happened.

I remember being invited to give a keynote speech at the World Trade Center on 17 September 2001. On the 11th of September, as we all know, a group of terrorists crashed into both of the World Trade Center buildings. I was amazed at the intensity with which the local organizers of this event were still sending me e-mails days later on how we could keep this date by simply finding a suitable new venue. Eventually the e-mails stopped, but only after the organizers had gone through the slow process of digesting the enormity of what had occurred.

I had a similar experience during a course I was teaching in Bamako, Mali when an Icelandic volcano and its explosive clouds of ash paralyzed most of Europe's air traffic. I was surprised by the insistent calls from the employers of some of my stranded European colleagues, telling them that they needed to find their way back to the office immediately. Again, these narrow-minded or ill-informed superiors lacked the short-term ability to gauge the scale of the problem.

I believe that the same kind of mental buffers are at play when we cannot grasp the magnitude of a catastrophe as when we fail to see the magnitude of the opportunities around us. Both are the result of a relatively closed mind.

The road-less-traveled is a lonely and risky route to take. However, it is often the one most worthwhile. For me, as

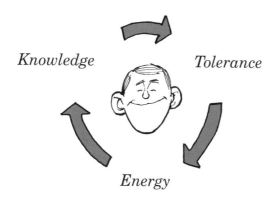

FIGURE 1-1: **The virtuous circle of the open mind**

a North American, Finland was off the radar screen and clearly off the beaten path. Nothing in my life experience or heritage indicated that I would ever think of coming to this country. I am glad today to have had the open-mindedness to consider moving here. My Finnish life-venture has, like Finland itself, been quite extraordinary.

Several factors help us to maintain an open mind. Among the most significant are:

- A good **knowledge** base
- A **tolerance** for diversity
- **Energy**

These three elements form the necessary parts of a causal chain for sustaining an open mind. Though we all know very little from the infinite body of available information, the more we learn, the more we are able and often willing to learn. A good knowledge foundation is thus the best springboard into the unknown. The acquisition of knowledge is also a contagious phenomenon in many developed societies. The more knowledge is acquired, the more people and their communities are able to stretch their cognitive boundaries.

An important factor in the efficient acquisition of knowledge is an open and flexible attitude towards information and people. The less dogmatic and the more inclusive we are, the smarter we become. This means that the knowledge acquisition process should be as fluid, democratic and untainted as possible. When emotional, factional or otherwise political buffers narrow the scope of what the mind has to play with, our minds atrophy and our ventures suffer.

A particularly impressive display of flexible thinking and agile policy-making was demonstrated by one of the country's greatest political icons, President Urho Kekkonen. His story and contribution to the Finnish post-war miracle are covered in the text-box of this section.

Finally, the practice of keeping an open mind requires effort and energy. This is not a natural habit for many adults. As our childlike curiosity fades, our practice of putting our world into question diminishes drastically. For many of us, just getting by with the knowledge we have acquired is challenging enough. However, we find that those who maintain the fire of learning throughout their days, or who push themselves along the path of knowledge, live fuller lives. They also tend to have already covered the first stage of miracles-in-the-making. Their mind is open and their propensity to succeed is relatively higher than it is for learning laggards.

Finns are known for their reserved communication style. Because of this, many outsiders come to the conclusion that Finns are not very open-minded. People from Western cultures often take silence as a sign of lack of interest or lack of imagination.

In fact, Finns are actually more open-minded than may appear to the casual observer. Generally speaking, Finns are very well-educated. They are reasonably tolerant and hard working and thus keep a fairly positive mindset. In fact, under some international surveys, Finland has been found to be among the happiest nations on earth.[1] I examine these national traits and these three drivers of open-mindedness in greater detail in the following sections.

URHO
the wise
and the post-war
miracle

Urho Kaleva Kekkonen is undoubtedly the dominant political figure of Finland's post-war history. He served as Prime Minister of Finland from 1950 to 1953 and then again from 1954 to 1956. He later became the eighth President of Finland for a commanding term of 26 years (1956 to 1982). The son of land-owning farmers, he ultimately obtained his law doctorate from the University of Helsinki. He was also an enthusiastic sportsman and was the 1924 Finnish high-jump champion. He was born in the Savo region of Finland, an Eastern province near Russia.

Kekkonen came from a fervently anti-communist background. During the Finnish Civil War of 1918, he fought in the conservative White Guard and is even believed to have led some of the brutal firing squads against communist fighters during this difficult period of Finnish history. Paradoxically, in his later life, he is credited with the building of an excellent political relationship with the Soviet leadership.

Indeed, towards the end of the Continuation War (1941 to 1944), Urho Kekkonen was one of the first politicians to actively engage in the development of ties with the Soviet government. For Finland, it was paramount to implement a rapid change of leadership from those who, like President Risto Ryti, had been strongly aligned with Nazi Germany in the war effort, and to engage in a new era of peaceful cooperation with the Soviet Union. Kekkonen was at the forefront of this initiative. This important period of Finnish history is discussed in greater detail in the chapter of this book dealing with *sisu*.

Kekkonen's background as a Minister of the Agrarian League (later renamed the Center Party) gave him credibility in the Soviets' eyes, since he came from the heartland of Finland and, though being center-conservatives, members of this party were still seen as the representatives of a vast working farmer population which was ideologically tolerable to the Soviets. He later continued what was called the policy of "active neutrality" of President Juho Paasikivi, which came to be known as the "Paasikivi-Kekkonen line."

This policy allowed Finland to retain its independence and trade with the nations of NATO and the Warsaw pact. In international policy circles this approach to foreign affairs was given an attention-grabbing name: *Finlandization*. The term came from German political scientists, but was mostly resented in Finland. It was perceived as a critique of the country's Realpolitik, which had been designed to allow Finland to tread safely on the coattails of an unpredictable and powerful neighbor.

From the perspective of this book and the Possibility Model, Urho Kekkonen is perhaps one of the great masters of the open mind and the father of the Finnish post-war social-economic miracle. Despite his rural roots, Kekkonen dedicated much of his life to learning and ultimately becoming a Doctor of Laws. His knowledge base and ability to absorb new information were thus at a high level. His display of tolerance and flexibility in diplomacy was admirable. He could move from being a staunch anti-communist to becoming the friend of the Soviet leadership and still retaining the independence of his country. Overall, this was one of the great political feats of the last century. His persistence and ability to maintain this course throughout his 26 year term is nothing less than extraordinary.

His intelligent and flexible policy laid the foundation for one the great Finnish miracles. The post-war period in Finland was perhaps the most dramatic occurrence of class-less social-economic growth in history.[2] The war reparations paid by Finland to the Soviet Union were harsh. However, Finland is the only country in post-war Europe to have paid its debt back in full. One of the reasons for this is that it was in Finland's long-term interest to do so.

The country needed to industrialize quickly to create the manufacturing goods that the terms of the debt required. To meet this challenge, sudden and massive investments in the metal industry, the ship-building industry and forestry technology were made. This, in turn, developed the back-bone of a modern industrial nation able to trade with all nations regardless of their political alignment during the Cold War. Kekkonen and those politicians who worked to build and maintain this relative-neutrality policy thus gave Finnish industry a miraculous opportunity to have the best of a world divided in two.

Many would smile at the author's portrayal of Urho Kek-konen as an open-minded leader. To some of his critics in Finland, he was a first-class authoritarian. Many years after his death, there was a good deal of debate in the national media about the appropriateness of his seemingly undemocratic maneuverings. For the purposes of this book, it suffices to mention that keeping an open mind is not synonymous with systematically taking all opinions into account. At some point it becomes imperative to make up one's mind and act accordingly. Kekkonen's open mind needs to be acknowledged from the perspective of the times in which he lived and the flexibility of mind and action that he allowed himself to develop in relation to his own ideological background.

1.2 The ruthless egalitarian

As stated above, tolerance is at the core of an open mind. No matter how well-endowed we are with information and knowledge, our ability to accept another point of view or integrate a different type of thinker into a group is vital to keeping our minds open and achieving success.

For this reason, we find that egalitarian and inclusive societies are often open-minded and successful societies. When the laws and the culture of a nation strongly integrate minorities or weaker societal groups, this stimulates tolerance and promotes free and open thinking.

In its short history, Finland has had a decent record in practicing social tolerance and integration. The Finnish culture of social integration finds its roots in the lifestyle of Finns throughout their history. The need to be highly cooperative and use every available human resource was and still is critical in a sparsely populated country faced with unpredictable weather conditions.

The political and economic evolution of Finland explains its exceptionally egalitarian way of operating. Until 1917, Finland was under Russian rule, and prior to 1809 the territory known today as Finland was part of the kingdom of Sweden for several hundred years. One result of this long governance by foreign powers is the lack of an indigenous aristocracy and complex class structure. After the Second World War, most of the Finnish population was poor and most of the economy still based on agriculture. One of the Finnish miracles was the extraordinary growth of a hefty middle class fueled by rapid industrialization and high-quality education. Partly because of this, most Finns strongly feel that they are socially equal to each other.

This forms a striking contrast with other Western and even other Nordic countries. In Finland, it is not unusual for subordinates to openly criticize the views and actions of management. Heads of major corporations, government ministers and other high-profile individuals are surprisingly accessible to the public. Nothing is frowned upon more in Finland than a condescending communications style or an unduly hierarchical organization.

The Finnish wage and tax structures are based upon ferociously egalitarian precepts. Wage scales in most Finnish companies are much narrower that in other Western economies. The progressive taxation is particularly leveling, with percentages going up to a nearly 60 percent marginal tax rate for higher income brackets. Only a few countries in the world match Finland in this regard. The result is that a very large part of the population makes roughly the same income. By the same token, all of the impressive social services and support systems are indiscriminately available to all.

Another interesting feature of Finnish egalitarianism is every person's right to public access to the wilderness. Based on an age-old Nordic tradition, this custom gives every person the right to access land which is in principle private property. Surprisingly, much of this right is based on custom and the general legal principle *nulla poena sine lege*, which means that what is not strictly forbidden is permitted. Over the years, the legislature has come to somewhat restrict this right, in order to preserve natural habitats and avoid undue nuisance to landowners; still, the exercise of the right has remained relatively widespread compared to similar rights granted in other countries.

The main reason for this is that Finnish rural societies never adopted feudalism or serfdom. In addition, as in Sweden and Norway, large unenclosed areas of forests have escaped the legal trappings of strict private ownership. This remnant of rights from times past gives some additional insight into the Finland of today. Equality is so engrained in the Finnish psyche that even the land, though vested in private ownership, is still accessible to all.

The culture and practice of the Finnish *talkoot,* or a community "pitch-in," is a great national tradition and example of cooperative inclusiveness. The main idea behind a *talkoot* is close to the traditional barn-raising culture in rural America. Finland urbanized later than many Western countries, mostly during the 1950s, and so this rural practice is still very much part of the culture even in the bigger cities. In a *talkoot,* all members of a community are asked and expected to give their contribution to a joint effort. All types of work and all people are a valued part of the collaborative chain. Once someone has called a *talkoot* for his or her benefit, the natural expectation is that he or she shall participate in future *talkoots* called by others.

Classic examples of a massive Finnish cooperative effort are the wars fought against the Soviet Union in 1939 and 1941. All Finns, regardless of politics, gender, religion or native tongue, were mobilized in this heroic David-and-Goliath-like struggle with a much larger nation. We cover this Finnish miracle, a critical part of the nation's history, in greater detail in the chapter on *sisu.* For now it is enough to note that the wars gave Finns the telling adage: "Kaveria ei jätetä." This literally means that a friend should never be left behind. This popular Finnish expression still pops up in conversations today and demonstrates the importance given to protecting each member of the community and thus keeping all possible human resources available for the fulfillment of a common objective.

Perhaps one of the most impressive modern examples of Finnish cooperative problem solving is the creation of the Linux operating system. It was a humble student at the

University of Helsinki, Linus Torvalds, who first wrote the Linux kernel, which later became one of the world's most important open-source operating systems. Torvalds was simply frustrated with the commercial restrictions attached to the existing operations systems he needed. He thus decided to begin writing his own and invited anyone else in the world to freely use and improve it. The result has been a global *talkoot* which generated the pillars of the Internet and a multi-billion-dollar software industry.

Neither she nor he

One of the most striking areas of social egalitarianism in Finland is in the area of gender equality. Finland was the second country in the world and the first country in Europe to give women the right to vote. Today, Finnish politics are a real reflection of a nation where women wield as much political and societal power as men. Even the Finnish language quite characteristically does not have a word for distinguishing between "he" and "she." Finnish only has the word *hän*, which can mean either a man or a woman.

On two occasions in Finland's recent history, both the President of the Republic and the Prime Minister have been women serving at the same time. Half of the ministers of the past few governments have been women. In fact, as well as being the first European country to give women the right to vote, Finland was the first country in the world where women could also stand for election, starting in 1906. Generally, Finnish women have taken their place in traditionally more masculine occupations, at construction sites, in taxis, in the army and in the boardroom. Though the issue of equal pay and the poor representation of women in power positions of the private sector are still part of a sometimes heated national debate, the practice of gender equality in Finland has been pushed much further than in most countries of the world.

Diversity stimulates the mind, creates dynamic pools of human resources and creates the best possible base for achieving success. Empowering women throughout all levels of society, in effect half of the national population, is clearly conducive to increasing economic efficiency and competitiveness.[3] When the competence pool of a country is wide and deep, the dynamics of the work market improve and produce positive economic and societal results. In illustration of these advantages, the following chapters contain some inspiring success stories of Finnish women.

A tale of two tongues

Since its inception in 1917, Finland has officially been a bilingual country. Today, the Finnish-speaking Finns represent the majority of the population while the Swedish-speaking Finns represent a bit more than 5 percent of the population. Neither the integration of these two national cultures nor the co-existence between the two linguistic groups has been without its trials.

The Swedish-speaking minority of Finland has often been perceived by the majority of Finns as a well-endowed and elitist group. Indeed, in proportion to its size, this group has wielded a considerable amount of economic and political power. Despite the language confrontations of the past, Finns in general have been able to use this diversity to their advantage. The critical relationships with Sweden and the rest of the Nordic countries have certainly been reinforced by the maintenance of and proficiency in a common Nordic language. The political, military and economic evolution

of Finland is heavily marked by the ties and assistance it has received from its Nordic neighbors throughout its short national history. In turn, Swedish-speaking Finns have been culturally defined by their Finnish-speaking compatriots as distinct and different from Sweden and other Nordic countries where languages closer to Swedish are spoken.

In the opinion of Sophie Mannerheim, the sister of war hero and national leader Marshal C. G. E. Mannerheim, the existence of the two linguistic communities of Finland is a defining part of the national identity. In the late twenties, she was a famous Swedish-speaking Finn and was one of the best-known women of the nation's early history.

"The meeting and even the fighting between the country's two cultures," she stated, "triggered the spark that gave the Finnish nation its particular ingenuity. For this reason Finland's culture is richer than other countries' cultures. Without you, the Finnish-speaking Finns, we would be ordinary Swedes. Through you we have become Finns who believe in being ourselves and feel at home only in Finland. Finnish-speaking Finns need Swedish-speaking Finns just as much, so as not to lose the country's special edge."[4]

This kind of thinking ultimately produced a national understanding on language, an understanding that made Finland stronger from within. It created a like-minded and united people who could better withstand the pressure and suffering of war and the building of a strong democracy.

I see the same challenges and opportunities in Finland's bilingualism as in the bilingualism of my native country of Canada. In Canada, our bilingualism differentiates us from the United States and our integration and dynamic interaction between cultures increases our strength as a nation. English-speaking Canada makes the French-speaking province of Québec stronger in the face of a powerful English-speaking continent. English-speaking Canada is stronger because it can more clearly differentiate itself from our common southern neighbor. The challenge of cultural diversity is an invitation to grow stronger as people and as nations.

Mad about metal

An interesting aspect of Finnish open-mindedness can be seen in its acceptance and encouragement of niche and sometimes strange sub-cultures. Consider, for instance, the rise of Finnish hard rock and metal music.

Finland has a rich musical heritage. Music education has been strongly encouraged throughout the country's short history. Finland has produced the likes of Jean Sibelius, Oskar Merikanto and many other prominent composers. More recently, Finland has generated a stunning set of world-class opera singers and conductors. In relation to the country's size, these achievements on the world's classical music scene are considerable.

On the popular music front, however, the global pickings have been slim. It is only at the beginning of the new millennium that Finnish bands have come into their own.

Among the most innovative and internationally acclaimed are bands that have leveraged Finnish classical musical strengths and combined them with the hard rock genre. Nightwish originally featured a classically trained performer, Tarja Turunen, as its lead singer. Apocalyptica is a group of cellists who began their careers by doing instrumental covers of bands such as Metallica and have now carved a solid place for themselves in the history of metal music.

One of the maddest manifestations of Finnish culture and a testament to the open-mindedness of the nation is the epic story of Lordi. Their unique approach to hard rock entertainment and their national and international achievements are recounted in the text-box of this section.

The pride and prejudice of LORDI

The story of Lordi begins far in the north of Finland, near the city of Rovaniemi. A young man called Tomi Putaansuu is fascinated with bands like KISS that combine rock music with extravagant masks, make-up and costumes. Putaansuu is a true fan of this genre and decides to raise it up a few notches with his own original concept.

The young Putaansuu starts developing his music and the characters that will bring it to life. The main figure of the band, which he incarnates, is Mr. Lordi, a towering medieval ogre with the face of a frightening monster and the body of medieval soldier straight out of *The Lord of the Rings*. A sense of revolution and fear is part of the entertainment experience. The other characters in the band are just as amusingly repulsive as Mr. Lordi himself. The band produces some very decent hard rock music, its strong visual presence punctuated with exciting pyrotechnics. Mr. Lordi is definitely not among the most accomplished of hard rock or heavy metal singers, but his voice fits the special needs of the genre.

Like many Finnish legends, Lordi was born out of a challenging national situation. In the case of Lordi, it was Finland's systematic humiliation at the Eurovision song contest. Though this event may not register on the radar screen of people outside Europe, it is a big deal for many Europeans and for the European music industry. Every year since 1961 Finland has sent its artists to represent the country in this song contest. The goal of Eurovision is to promote European culture and create a sense of pride in the continent's music traditions in the midst of the widely dominant American popular music culture. Some of the better-known names to have won the competition are ABBA from Sweden and Céline Dion from Canada. Though Canada is not a European country, the rules of competition have stated that only one of either the composer, writer or performer need to be from the participating country of the European Broadcasting Area. Céline Dion represented Switzerland in 1988 and won.

In 2006, Finland had participated in the Eurovision song contest a total of 44 times and had never taken home the main prize. The country's best performance dated back to 1973, when Marion Rung placed a decent sixth in the contest. This serial under-performance had given rise to a fatalistic humor spree every year. Many Finns, when talking about the event, would humorously utter "Finlande: 0 point!" in broken French hinting at Eurovision's bilingual TV format and the sad results Finland had to endure over the years.

One of the main challenges of the contest is also its greatest opportunity. Many top European acts traditionally stay away from the event. A little bit like the European parliament, Eurovision tends to collect the music industry's "wannabes" or "has-beens." For the high-flying music stars of Europe, an appearance on the Eurovision song contest is often seen as a downgrade. This explains why England, for example, with its vast collection of international music stars, has not performed well in this event. They just don't send their most famous artists. For Finland, the main success stories of the last decade, such as HIM or the Rasmus, have also stayed away. This state of affairs allows Eurovision to serve as a special springboard for the still relatively unknown.

Given the challenging history of national failure at this event, Finland decided to seriously reform its Eurovision selection process in 2005. First, the major record companies were invited to submit their best artists. Second, the voting process was submitted to the television audience rather than to the old appointed panel of connoisseurs from YLE, the National Broadcaster of Finland.

In 2006, Sony BMG entered Lordi, probably the craziest-looking band most Finns had ever seen. The vast hard and metal rock fan base of Finland was mobilized. Also, the egalitarian and open culture operated in favor of pushing for a refreshing change. *Et voilà!* The Monsters were off to Athens to represent their country.

Lordi's entry created quite a stir in the local and European media. Everybody had an opinion. A genuine Finnish buzz developed in the international press prior to the event, and that is just what Finland and Lordi needed. The Monsters ended up winning the European title with a record amount of points. It was unbelievable. People invaded the streets much as they had done in 1995 when Finland for the first time won the Ice Hockey World Championships. The market square swelled up on 26 May 2006 with 90 000 Finns for a victory celebration concert and an award ceremony conducted by the President of the Republic, Tarja Halonen. It was unforgettable.

The Lordi story is, on its own scale, a Finnish miracle. First, the venture required an open mind. The people of Finland and the National Broadcaster had the broadmindedness to accept what would have been earlier deemed inappropriate. Mr. Lordi had been working on his concept since 1992 and the band was created as early as 1996. The road to this success was long and unclear and thus there was a good amount of trial and error involved. For a small country with limited access to global marketing funds, the introduction of an outrageous and novel idea was the smartest and most efficient way to trigger the needed media attention at a critical time. The fear of ridicule and the shame of a nation needed to be faced and a drastic change of format needed to be attempted. Finally, Mr. Lordi and his band were being powerfully themselves, in a tribute to Finnish authenticity. It wasn't just five musicians putting on masks at the last minute to generate media attention. These were artists of a genre to which they had dedicated most of their professional careers. And it showed.

Being bare

One of the most interesting features of Finnish culture is the wide appeal of the sauna. Finland, a country of 5.3 million people, boasts over three millions saunas. Indeed, saunas are everywhere. You find them in each apartment building or private dwelling, in most businesses, in some deep ore mines and even in the skyboxes of some ice hockey arenas.

The vast appeal of the sauna dates back to its role and function in Finnish rural history.

Distinguished by their utility and versatility, saunas were often built before the construction of the main house on one's property. The idea was that the sauna could serve as temporary living quarters during the construction phase. Indeed, the sauna could be used as a kitchen for cooking, a refuge from the cold temperatures and a bathing room for basic hygiene. In fact, the smoke from the sauna has been found to release tannic acid, an anti-bacterial polymer, ensuring a fairly sterile environment. For this reason and up until the mid-twentieth century, it was common practice for midwives to assist with births in the family sauna.

For all its functionality, I believe that perhaps the greatest contribution of the sauna to Finnish society lies in instilling a healthy attitude towards nudity and generating wide-spread open-mindedness. This is perhaps one of the most drastically different cultural aspects of Finnish life compared to most countries. Families are used to bathing together. Same-sex colleagues and friends are also used to going to the sauna together. From my point of view, this practice opens the mind of Finns and acts as a social equalizer and a distinctive catalyst for open and frank communication.

For someone outside of the culture there can be something shocking about socializing in the nude. For Finns it is a natural part of a party among friends or work colleagues. This may seem strange to the foreign reader, but it is somehow intrinsically positive to be naked in the sauna with your peers. The setting allows no place for pretenses, for hiding behind clothing as an attribute of power. In the sauna, all are equal and what you see is what you get: just another human being like you. At the psychological and even the spiritual level, I firmly believe that this practice is a driver for Finland's cooperative and cohesion-driven culture and perhaps one of the secrets of its social successes.

The Finnish wedding

Canadians like myself tend to think we are easygoing and tolerant people. Indeed we travel extensively, we usually speak more than one language, and our education system is also highly praised internationally. In many respects we are close to the Finnish state of mind. However, Finland can offer most foreigners, including Canadians, mind-stretching experiences.

I realized this when I was invited to a Finnish wedding for the first time. I was working at a summer high school in Suolahti, a small village in central Finland. The invitation came as a surprise, as I didn't know the married couple at all. It was my colleague and friend Heli who suggested I go with her and her husband Arvo for what she promised would be a memorable cultural experience.

I really didn't know what to expect. I put on the best clothes I could find from my limited tourist gear, and off I went to the wedding. It was a surprisingly colorful affair. The newlyweds were semi-professional folk dancers, so the celebrations were full of live folk music and extensive folk dancing in quaint blue, red and white costumes. The older and non-dancing guests were dressed in standard-issue tuxedos, dark suits or dresses. In between bouts of folk dancing, I attempted to make conversation with some of the locals with limited success. This is when my host Arvo came to ask me with typical Finnish directness: "André, are you bored?" I politely replied "Well, not really but…" to which he uttered a sharp "Come with me now."

He opened the door of a small cubicle in the main building of the country estate. As I was shutting the door behind me he surprised me by saying: "Take your clothes off." In the twenty-two years of life experience I had accumulated at that point, the only persons to have made that same explicit request had been a few nurses and my mother. I kept my cool and told him that he was a charming man but that I was mostly interested in women. He ignored my defensive resort to humor and simply repeated: "Take your clothes off." I quickly gave in and said to myself, "Oh well what's the worst that could happen?" He opened another door and we entered a shower room. It then became clear to me that we were going to go for a sauna session, albeit in the middle of a wedding.

This particular sauna was in some respects hotter than anything I had imagined: it had a naked woman in it. Yes, I was with a naked woman and a silent man during a traditional wedding. Truly exotic, and from my youthful and North American perspective paralyzingly exciting. I didn't know quite how to handle the situation, but as with most novel or shocking experiences I knew that rule number one is to keep your cool despite the heat.

After the initial short salutations "Hei," to which one responds "Hei," I dropped into an uncharacteristic silence. I started sweating heavily with my legs tightly crossed, unwilling to reveal myself in any way. Finally I broke the tension with something stupid like: "Ouf, so do you sweat here often? Oh! I mean is this usual? I mean traditional?..." Arvo rescued me from my tenuous babbling with a straight question: "Are you hot?" I answered an unequivocal: "Yes, I'm boiling." "Come with me," he said, and so I followed him promptly out of the sauna.

We took a short, cool shower and then Arvo led me through yet another door. This one led not to another part of the building, but <u>outside</u>. As I stepped into the cool, crisp Finnish air, I almost lost my breath from the realization that my good Arvo was taking me through the festivities in the nude. It was like a very bad dream that feels very real. No, this was really happening and I was keeping a stiff smile on my face as I walked and dripped my way through the folk dancers and the ladies with their big elegant hats. My host was not bothered and so I tried to say to myself "When in Rome..."

My aboriginal guide was taking me to the lake as part of an ancestral sauna ritual and maybe the need to give a young Canadian boy something to talk about back home. On the way back, I courageously saluted the wedding guests with my privates slightly affected by the surprisingly cold water. "Hello, hello. Great wedding!" I said while thinking that I hoped I would never see any of them again. "Are you still bored?" asked Arvo returning to the sauna. "NO! Not anymore. Thank you."

The joke is on you

Humor is one of the great catalysts for open-mindedness. Through good wit, parody or exaggeration, one allows the mind to stretch and the soul to relax.

In Finland, the most popular form of humor is what I would call "egalitarian humor." Finns enjoy making fun of people in positions of power. Perhaps one of the clearest examples of this is the massive popularity of Conan O'Brien's series of sketches about the Finnish President, Tarja Halonen. O'Brien's first routines were based on his surprising facial resemblance to the first female Finnish President. This culminated in a rock-star-like welcome for the American comedian at the Helsinki-Vantaa airport and his official meeting with the President of the Republic. The Finnish President, who is known to be very close to the people, played along wonderfully, to the delight of the Finnish audience.

Another example of egalitarian humor is the unbelievable popularity of *Uutisvuoto*, a Finnish television show launched in Finland in 1998. The original format came from the UK's BBC and was called *Have I Got News for You*. It has been running since 1990 on the BBC airwaves, and likewise it is one of the Finnish national broadcaster's longest-running TV shows. Finns just love a good weekly slap of humor and satire aimed at high-profile individuals. The show thoroughly entertains and speaks to the deeply engrained sense of social equality.

Another greatly appreciated form of Finnish humor is self-irony or parody. This involves making fun of oneself or feeling comfortable with the fact that the joke is on you. A good example of this is the depiction of teachers in the book series Ella, written by a former teacher, Timo Parvela. The atmosphere in the stories is warm and funny. In 1998 Mr. Parvela won the President's award for favorite children's book. In the Ella stories, the teacher is often portrayed in a humorous manner. This does not stop these books being used in Finnish classrooms. Teachers, along with other persons in positions of power, easily accept being at the center of a good laugh. It is part of the Finnish egalitarian culture.

1.3 Education, education and education

When President Tarja Halonen is asked why Finland has been so successful in many international surveys,[5] her answer has often been the title of this section. A highly educated population is arguably the greatest resource a country can have. Indeed many of the countries that have been blessed with a great deal more national resources don't even come close to the Finnish figures obtained in the comparative analysis of national social and economic performance.

Finland has one of the best basic education systems in the world. This claim is clearly supported by several studies. The most important of these are the PISA (Programme for International Student Assessment) tests organized every three years since 2000. In each year the focus of the PISA tests is different. In 2003 and 2006 the focus was on mathematics and science respectively. In both those rounds of tests, Finland came in at number one. In the 2009 survey, Finland was a close second to South Korea in the national PISA scores. Indeed, many foreign education professionals have referred to this achievement as a Finnish miracle.[6]

In 2010, the positive results coming from such benchmark exercises prompted the Finnish Brand Delegation to make education one of the cornerstones of the Finnish brand. Under the assertive title "Finland gives you a lesson," the Country Brand Report[7] raises high performance in education as one of the country's main reputation attributes. It also claims that Finland's people and especially its teachers can be part of the solution for some of the world's most challenging problems.

Several countries' media outlets and groups of experts have visited Finland in an attempt to find out why Finns are so dominant in the field of basic education. To a great extent, the success of Finnish education is a manifestation of Finland's values and culture. The ruthless egalitarianism and the general trust of Finns in their institutions and in each other go a long way toward explaining these great results.

Throughout its history, Finland has made a series of positive strategic decisions with regards to education. Finns are reaping the benefits of this long and sustained pro-education policy today. In the mid 19th century, under the leadership of education visionaries such as J. V. Snellman and Uno Cygnaeus, Finns realized that a country with limited natural resources and a small population needed to make systematic investments into education in order to fare well in the global economy.

Legislation giving free and equal access to basic schooling and libraries was already a reality at the turn of the 20th century. This important principle was embedded in the first Finnish constitution of 1919. There are no private schools to speak of in Finland and the quality of teaching is high across the entire basic education system.

The egalitarian policy of the society in general has always been reflected in the overall education system. Many of the high profile leaders of the early republic were indeed from humble middle-class families. Gender equality in education was also present early on. A majority of university students have been women since the 1940's. In the PISA test, Finnish girls are often the differentiating factor in bringing the country to the top of the scale. In the 2009 PISA tests, Finnish girls outperformed the boys by the largest margin among all OECD countries.

As we shall see in the chapter on working harder and smarter, Finns excel in the application of the principle "less is more." This means that as far as reasonably possible, one should try to produce better results using fewer resources.

We shall look at well-known business and military examples of this Finnish propensity for high efficiency in later chapters. This efficiency pattern has also been at play in the administration of Finnish education.

Two examples of Finnish efficiency in dispensing education are particularly interesting. For example, in 2006, Finland spent under 7000 dollars per student for basic education. The equivalent figure for the USA in that year was 10 000 dollars. Finland ranked first in the PISA tests that year while the USA ranked 24th. Finland's expenditures for basic education are within the OECD average and yet its performance is among the world's best.

In the late 1950's, on the recommendation of the Finnish Teacher Association of Foreign Languages (SUKOL), it was decided that foreign movies and television series should only be subtitled, instead of dubbed as is common in many other European countries. At that time, the high cost of producing quality dubbing for a relatively small population encouraged this decision. However, the positive educational effects of the decision were also part of the thinking at the time. In the end, the educational impact on national literacy and proficiency in foreign languages has been dramatic. Compared to their continental European peers, Finns master foreign languages significantly better and are among the most literate and educated populations in the world.

Additional explanations for Finland's superior results in basic education can be found in other areas of life. As in many successful large corporations and organizations, the Finnish education system has found the right balance between central control and regional adaptation. The system is uniform at the national level and the core curriculum sets the standards for all schools. However, local schools receive a substantial amount of flexibility and autonomy so as to adapt to the particular circumstances of specific localities.

In addition, the Finnish culture of inclusiveness is most definitely present in the school system. Special needs and the general welfare of students are efficiently addressed. The school's staff and the wider community have several communication and support mechanisms that allow all stakeholders to make a contribution to the national education process.[7]

The secrets of play

I remember taking my children home from our local day care and kindergarten and being worried about the "curriculum" followed by the teachers. I definitely had an old-fashioned Canadian and continental European prejudice relating to this question. I thought to myself: "Oh those Finnish teachers are much too passive. They should be more hands-on with those 3 to 5 year-olds. They should take advantage of the time they have to begin with reading and writing exercises!"

I was also a little worried by the fact that my children had continuously the same thing to say to me when I picked them up. "What did you do today, sweetheart?" "I played, Daddy." "Did you LEARN anything today?" "No, we just played," my 4-year-old daughter would say.

This, I told myself, was a far cry from the Italian nuns who had the first go at my education when I was their age. What I remember from my early education is a strict bunch of well-intentioned ladies in dark gowns giving out stern lectures and some light physical punishment for misbehaving children. In this context, the concept of play was closely associated with futile leisure and completely dissociated from the concept of education. At the tender age of four, we had proper classes that rather rigidly introduced us to the written word.

This was, and still is for many, including myself, the recipe for life-long success. Work as hard and as seriously as you can and you shall succeed in life. Luckily for me, I was kicked out of the Italian nun's school for insubordination. Thinking back to that time, I realized that many of my friends from the private nuns' kindergarten never made it to college. With my new start in the public school system, I ended up having a long and happy stay at a few universities around the world some twenty years later.

This is by no means a scientific analysis of the efficiency of strict and old-fashioned Catholic education methods versus the more modern and secular approaches of the Nordic countries. I have, however, come to believe that an important part of the success of the Finnish basic education system is in the freedom it allows during the early years.

Finns believe that children should be given a chance to be children before they become students. I remember expressing my concern about that lack of "work" done in daycare to my wise Finnish wife. "Honey, shouldn't they be doing something instead of just playing?" I used to say. "They ARE doing something. They are playing. THAT is their job."

I didn't realize it then, but I see it now more clearly. Already at this stage of the game, Finns play fairer and smarter. By letting their children be children, they create the basis for academic success. When they come to the phase of more formal education (6 to 7 years old), most Finnish children are still excited about school. In certain other cultures such as France, England or Italy, some pupils are already fed up with school and lose interest at the outset of what should normally be a long and exciting journey. Some children may indeed feel that they have been, to a certain extent, robbed of their childhood and their right to play, and thus resent formal schooling for the rest of their lives.[9]

Another key aspect of the Finnish education system is its flexibility. In many parts of the world the education culture is tainted by values of competition and rather brutal efficiency. This is mostly true in countries like Japan, the USA and other highly competitive social cultures. The traditional education model of these countries is tailored to fit the industrial societies it was meant to serve. The education system is like a fast-rotating factory belt. Those who manage to stay on will eventually be sold as premium products, and those who couldn't stay on are swept into the social waste bin. In many ways, traditional Western schooling is a reflection of our highly competitive global marketplace.

Finnish education has by no means been sheltered from the forces of competition and specialization required by the traditional labor markets. However, these forces have been somewhat tempered by values that have allowed the country to make better use of its human resources.

The Finnish education system is well-balanced in terms of its content. In addition to a solid curriculum and successful measures to promote literacy, mathematical skills and basic knowledge of science, the education system equally and widely promotes things like music education, physical activity and closeness to nature. It may be argued that the balance between the *hard* and the *soft* contents of Finnish education is mutually supportive. *Mens sana in corpore sano* is a classic adage that has not gone unaddressed in the Finnish school system.

The school system's flexibility also manifests itself in both the timing and financing of education. High school in Finland, for example, can be done entirely at night school at any given age. Full school years or some particular courses can always be redone so students have the chance to achieve better scores and enter a better program in institutions of higher learning. Once students reach the institutions of higher learning, their attendance at classes and the administration of their exams can be coordinated to meet their special needs and schedules.

Finally, for more than three decades, all university students have received basic financial funding to be able to sustain themselves throughout the 5 to 6 years of their higher education. There are only minimal administration fees for attending university and most books can be found in ample supply for each course at the university library. As a teacher at the University of Jyväskylä, it always made me smile to hear my students complain about their perceived lack of resources during their studies. From a North American perspective, every single Finnish citizen is in fact on a full 6-year scholarship, with few debts incurred during the process. From this viewpoint, Finnish students are particularly fortunate.

The huge investment in free, fair and flexible basic and higher education ensures that Finland can make relatively more of the talent that exists in each one of its citizens. Perhaps the Japanese or the Americans can afford to apply a more closed and Darwinian scheme for academic success. Finns are more of a scarce commodity. This is why it is a better strategy to give more chances at academic success.

In his book *The Outliers*[10], Malcolm Gladwell supports this theory of wrongful exclusion. He posits the idea that many talented persons get excluded from opportunities for the wrong reasons. In competitive sports for instance, the highly competitive and discriminatory selection process was found to perpetuate the success of those who were born at a certain time of year. The selection system was found to unduly discriminate against those who were born on the early side of a given cut-off date. For instance, if a child were born at the end of December, he or she basically had little chances of being successful in competitive sports because players in their peer group had up to several months of physical maturity and thus a purely physiological age-based advantage in that particular group. This means that the selection system often mistook maturity for talent.

The Finnish education system does a better job of tackling unfair advantages, and allows everyone with the talent and the will to continue trying to let their academic or vocational talents shine through at some point in their life. In the eyes of some, this may be perceived as a waste of time and resources. In practice, it has worked as a talent optimization scheme triggered by a fair and flexible education policy.

Though the Finnish higher education system is fair, it is also competitive. Entrance exams are demanding. A place to study is earned and thus ensures sufficient motivation among the students. An interesting comparison is the case of France. In theory, the French higher education system is perhaps one of the most accessible and fair-minded in the world. Free access to higher education is a constitutional right. This typically causes French universities to take in three to four times the amount of people they can actually physically absorb in the first year of each new entering class of students.

The practice takes a catastrophic toll on the universities' physical and human resources. During the first year, the main objective of the institution is to cut down the classes to a manageable size for the second year. The result is a very low-performing public university system. The only way to gain access to top-quality higher education in France is to attend expensive private institutes of higher learning. In this interesting comparison between two types of educational socialism, the Finnish model seems to work better.

1.4 Still room for a stretch

However open-minded we think we are, there is always still room to stretch our minds and our imagination. Finns are no exception to this. We have seen how Finnish society and Finns in general possess an openness of mind that sets an excellent foundation for success in many fields. In this final section of the chapter, we take up some areas where the Finnish collective mind could use some widening, so as to ensure a better basis for success and perhaps some further Finnish miracles.

An open mind behind a closed door

As we have seen, most Finns are open-minded. They are highly educated, fairly tolerant and have a good work ethic. The coming decade shall, however, bring new challenges on the social tolerance front. In the late 80's, less than 1 percent of the population was made up of foreigners. Today, that number has risen to 3 percent of the population.

Almost half of this immigration has come from nearby countries, so the cultural differences have been relatively easy to manage. In addition, Finland is one of the European countries with the smallest number of foreign nationals living on its soil. However, the projections show a rapidly growing foreign population in some areas of Finland. In the capital area of Helsinki, it is predicted that by the year 2020 over 15 percent of the population may come from abroad. This new growth of foreigners living in Finland is partly fueled by the need for Finland to attract a young and capable workforce from other countries.

There are several reasons for the relative cultural homogeneity of Finland. First, the origins of the country and the main ancient migrations from the rest of the European continent have produced a fairly cohesive and stable gene pool. The theories of the origins of the Finnish people are many.[11] The slow migrations and Finland's relative geographic insularity have produced a social and ethnic fabric that has remained relatively unchanged over time.

Second, the latter half of the last century was marked by a developing industrial economy and an international low-profile policy. This was not a lure for any significant influx of new blood. In fact, many visitors to Finland during this period may have been left with a slightly negative perception of Finland. At the end of his stay as the United Kingdom's Ambassador to Finland, Sir Bernard Ledwidge, had this to say about the Finland of 1972:

> You would argue that for anyone other than a Finn, it is a disaster to spend three years in Finland, as I have just done. Finland is flat, cold and far from the busy centres of European life. Nature has not favoured Finland, nor has art for that matter.
>
> Up until recent times, the residents of Finland have included peasants, hunters, fishermen, and a small group of foreign rulers who spent most of their money elsewhere. The rich cultural history of Europe has left fewer marks in Finland than anywhere else in the Western world, perhaps excluding Iceland, Finnish cuisine deserves an extra punishment for its barbaric dreadfulness, only the mushrooms and the crawfish are worth mentioning.

Sir Ledwidge's view of Finland was clearly not endearing. Again, some of the trappings of the closed mind were certainly at play in his judgment. He, like many others, neglected to take into account where the country was coming from and perhaps more importantly where it was possibly going.

Finally, today's successful Finland is still largely an acquired taste for most visitors and foreign residents. The language is part of the Finno-Ugric family of languages, together with Hungarian and Estonian. Phonetically, it is as remote from other European languages as is Arabic or Japanese. This is a significant barrier to social entry.

The weather can also be considered harsh. After all, most of the world's people expect temperatures higher than 0 degrees Celsius, and crave more than four hours of light in the depths of winter. Add to this some of the highest taxes in the world and very few established ethnic communities and you obtain a decent explanation for relative Finnish ethnic homogeneity. Today's immigration to Finland is perhaps at the same stage as it was in the rest of Europe during the last century and in North America in the century before that.

Given this background, it was amusing to hear some of the arguments made during the early nineties against the country's entry into the EU. According to some of the tenets of the no vote, the yes vote victory would have opened the flood gates and the country would have been swamped by social-security-seeking foreigners. Needless to say, this did not happen. Finland ultimately entered the EU in 1995. The number of immigrants coming in from the EU at that time was minimal.

The social and economic barriers to entering Finland are still very high. There is now much debate over the potential problem of the labor shortage that shall hit Finland once the baby boomers have left for relatively early retirement. Many would like to address the problem by raising the retirement age. This alone will probably not suffice to fix the problem. Finland, more than most Western countries, is thus facing a historic demographic challenge. In 2011, Finland will become the first country in the EU to have fewer people entering the workforce than leaving it.

The challenges posed by Finland's need to attract and integrate foreigners present significant opportunities for the future. If done wisely, Finland can face the new challenges of globalization with greater confidence and insight than it holds today. Though Finland has once performed the economic miracle of transforming itself from an agrarian society into a first-class industrial economy in less than 50 years, it shall have to do something similar in the near future.

The world is becoming more competitive than ever. If once Finns believed that they can afford to lose some low-value factory work to developing countries as long as research and development activities remain in Finland, this view needs to be revised, and quickly. The developing world is now ready to play an ever stronger role in the high-value work needed by industry. Finland must increase its readiness to compete and improve at all levels of the industrial value chain. For this, it needs to leverage its strengths but also tackle some of its weaknesses.

Coming from Canada, I have seen and experienced the challenges and opportunities brought by immigration. Canada is one of the most open countries in the world. It has immigrants from literally all parts of the globe and has done one of the best jobs in using this to its advantage. One can see immigrants in all walks of life and at every level of the corporate hierarchy. Such workplace integration is still many years away for Finland.

Homogeneity in a given society definitely has its advantages. In terms of facilitating communication and work efficiency, a similar set of values, cultural references and ways of doing things certainly makes things run smoother and faster. Finnish society and its working community have clearly benefited from this.

One good example of seamless consensus-building can be seen in modern Finnish politics. Indeed, Finnish politics and the political media are surprisingly consensus-driven compared to their European or North American counterparts. Consider the so-called "rainbow coalition" of the Paavo Lipponen governments from the end of the 1990s and early 2000s, and the current "six-pack" coalition of Jyrki Katainen's government. The broad-based coalition included the social democrats, the leftist federation and the conservative coalition party, all in the same government.

This kind of functional multiparty governance is rare by any democratic standard. Perhaps because of the similar ethnic and educational backgrounds of most Finns, the colors of the Finnish political rainbow often appear as a variation in the shades of gray to the outside observer.

For all its challenges, immigration offers the potential for opening up the social debate and instilling new and innovative thinking in society and in business. According to a recent study, immigrants tend to be more creative than their resident peer group.[12] This is intuitively understandable since a new entrant to an established group usually needs to work harder and find new ways to operate in order to establish a place as a contributor to the group.

According to another study conducted in several Finnish multinational companies[13], Finns were ranked relatively poorly in their abilities to work fluidly with their non-Finnish colleagues. This has lot to do with the cultural assumptions that exist in all working processes. A typical Finnish worker will never have had to explain what he assumes to be self-evident from the commonly held "correct Finnish" way of understanding and doing things. One may argue that as we are exposed to different ways of doing things, we are in a better position to innovate. This is the great opportunity brought on by immigration and a key issue for Finland's future.

In many Finnish companies, the quest for efficiency and ever leaner processes are the specialty of management. Indeed, the engrained notion and value of "less is more"

FIGURE 1-2:

The Relativity Model of Efficiency to Creativity in Innovation

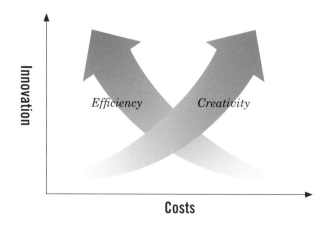

has led most Finnish companies to their relative successes. One of the secrets of Nokia's early success was indeed in manufacturing efficiency and logistics devised by some of the top engineers in the country. In terms of bold creativity, Finnish companies have lagged behind slightly. In the case of Nokia and the once hyper-expansive Sonera, the creativity of the likes of Apple, Skype and Google have delivered a hard blow to their market share.

Figure 1-2 represents the relationship between creativity and efficiency in relation to costs and innovation. The main point of the slide is that all four of these factors are connected. The relative level of creativity in running a business often relates to costs savings and innovation in a diametrically opposed way to the relative level of efficiency. In fact, their two curves often behave much like traditional supply and demand curves crossing each other from completely different directions.

The trick is to find the optimal point at which a business can get the most innovation out of its workforce in relation to the existing efficiency and creativity curves of the business. For many Finnish companies an influx of creative new blood from abroad could be just what is needed to shift the creativity curve up towards the left and thus promote both more innovation and lower operational costs.

My foreign husband is an idiot

This is the story of a freshly arrived North American father of two young children. His charming Finnish wife was frenetically preparing their new Finnish home for their first traditional Finnish Christmas. This involves a thorough cleaning of their home, the preparation of specific types of pastries and cookies, packing gifts and of course decorating the home. Being a typically efficient likes-to-work-alone Finnish wife, she only delegates to her husband a task that she thinks he can handle. She tells him that the house needs to be decorated with some Christmas elves. She gives him red cardboard, tape and some scissors. She asks him to involve the kids and says that she can put the elves up when she comes back from the grocery store.

The newly arrived father and husband looks at the red cardboard, the tape and scissors and rubs the back of his head a few times. The kids are quite new at this too, because they have never had a Christmas in Finland before. "Okay, kids," he says, "I have got a great idea for some really cool Christmas elves." The kids smile and start emptying the kitchen drawers and part of the garage to come up with something that will blow Mom away. Upon his wife's return, the father says: "Close your eyes, sweetheart." When she opens her eyes, her face is paralyzed with disbelief. She then begins to cry. The rest of the family is stunned. They think they have done a great job of making Christmas elves out of red cardboard, aluminum foil and their two brand-new basketballs.

"You silly man, you idiot! Don't you even know how to make proper Christmas elves? You simply need to cut out a pattern from the red cardboard and then hang them up like a garland on the wall like EVERYBODY does!" screams a very tired Finnish mother. Apparently, there is only one way to make a Christmas elf, and it is the Finnish way because as we all know Santa is from Finland...

We are all equal: No exceptions

As we have seen, Finns are ruthlessly egalitarian. This is a deeply rooted feature that has produced widespread and positive social and economic development. Finns are easily sold on arguments that involve policies or entitlements that benefit large masses of people in a similar way. Once exceptions begin to be made for a chosen few, Finns instinctively become more refractory. In general, Finnish social and economic policy is excellent at tackling the base of the pyramid. Finnish policies rarely show the same enthusiasm for supporting elite groups or institutions that are at the top of the pyramid.

A case in point is the contrast between Finland's top performance in dispensing basic education and its relatively weak results in higher education. If Finland gets brilliant marks for the quality of its basic education according to the PISA test, it enjoys far from such world-class luster on the side of higher education. Indeed in most world university rankings[14] Finnish universities are quite far from the top positions. This problem was taken into consideration in the country's brand report. One proposed solution was the greater involvement in higher education on the part of the world-class practitioners living in Finland who were perhaps educated abroad in some of the top universities of the world. This is a noble if probably not a realistic proposal.

One recent radical reform for higher education has been the merger of some of the best separate universities into a single institution. The Aalto University combines three fine universities (The Helsinki School of Economics, The University of Art and Design Helsinki and the Helsinki University of Technology) in the hope that the pooling of resources and the positive stimulation across disciplines might improve

Finland's future rankings among the world's universities. In addition, the state withdrew from the bureaucratic structures of the universities and encouraged them to find private funding for their activities, to which the state would grant generous matching funds. This introduces an element of competition between universities which may foster better results in the highly competitive higher education market.

Many in the Finnish academic community have been taken aback by this and some may indeed suffer in the short term. In this regard, the Finnish state has made a bold move in creating a situation by which not all institutions may receive equal treatment. This in my opinion is a refreshing change: a sign of open-mindedness that recognizes that in some domains treating all protagonists equally is conducive to success whereas in other settings it is a formula for mediocrity.

A similarly important area where different treatment might be conducive to greater equality and success would be the treatment of young and innovative companies, i.e., start-ups. The Finnish paradox in this area is that Finland leads the world in R&D expenditures as a percentage of GDP. Finland puts close to 4 percent of its GDP into R&D. The only other two countries in the world investing more than this are Israel and Sweden. Curiously, start-up driven innovation in Finland has been relatively weak compared to start-up powerhouses such as Israel.

Most of the venture capital firms have either left Finland or stopped making investments in young innovative companies altogether.[15] There are many reasons for these failures. One general explanation is the low level of innovative and internationally focused entrepreneurship in Europe.[16] There is a clear stigma attached to business experimentation and failure compared to North America and Silicon Valley in particular. The entrepreneurs of Silicon Valley are very open-minded about failures and bankruptcies. They see these as stepping stones towards a successful venture, and most investors in turn consider past failures as good experience and a creator of valuable insight into the entrepreneur's next venture. With European cultures in general and Finnish culture in particular, such business failures are mostly a source of embarrassment and ultimately a reason for potential investors to refuse entrepreneurs a second chance. We shall take another look at this feature of the Finnish psyche in the next chapter, dealing with trial and error.

Mikael Jungner, the former CEO of the National Broadcasting Corporation (YLE) and a leading politician, believes that the lack of access to capital is one of the country's biggest challenges.[17] Because of this drying up of private venture money, the Finnish state has tried to intervene. At the time of this writing, apart from the usual friends, family and fools who would typically support entrepreneurs with initial seed investment, the only doors to knock on for Finnish entrepreneurs are the state-supported agencies.[18]

These well-intentioned organizations are doing important work for the development of new ideas and businesses that shall, one hopes, carry Finland into an affluent future, one that can sustain the egalitarian welfare state. However, as was the case for universities, state-funded organizations tend to be unduly bureaucratic and often lack the drive and insightful edge that exist in private venture organizations. This area needs urgently to be developed in Finland in order to make the most of the significant potential for innovation that Finns have to offer.[19]

CHAPTER 2
Trial and error

Error by error one discovers the entire truth.

Sigmund Freud

The ability to take risks and persevere is central to the notion of success. Achievement depends heavily on the first steps taken from the starting point of an open mind and then onto the more perilous fields of concrete action. If our minds are open and produce stellar, innovative ideas but our feet remain stuck in inaction, our dreams simply vanish on the wind. Even after we have hit the ground hard after some lofty inspiration, the market is often the force that decides whether we need to run a 100 meter dash or a full marathon before breaking the ribbon of success.

This chapter looks at the different types of trial and error and their impact on success. Finns generally share a set of special cultural features that have made some of their trials successful and have inhibited others. This chapter also presents some examples of Finnish risk-taking and perseverance.

The phrase "trial and error" generally refers to a process of experimentation and learning which involves a series of attempts and failures in the quest for a solution to a given problem. It is the passage from inspiration to action. The process shares many similarities with the scientific method, where hypotheses are set forth and then followed by long, laborious and objective trials of observation before the creation of any formal theory. Trial and error processes are generally a more simplified version of the rigorous scientific method. To use a musical analogy: if the scientific method is Mozart, then trial and error is Madonna.

2.1 The hierarchy of trial and error

Three elements play a significant part in successful trial and error processes. These are luck, analytical intelligence and insight. Figure 2-1 presents a hierarchy where each of these three important elements holds a central role at its particular level. Trial and error processes that rely mainly on luck, or on hit-and-miss attempts at successful outcomes, are at the bottom of this hierarchy. This approach is referred to here as random trial and error. It is based on mechanical trial iteration and the checking of a result's compliance with a set objective. Luck or pure randomness is the main driver of successful outcomes at this level.

Once we add elements of intelligence to the process such as research and reasoning, we move up to the next level: cognitive trial and error. In this process, the experimenters aim to narrow the scope of necessary trials using the best possible information on the likelihood of successful outcomes. Intelligence is the driver of cognitive trial and error. In business ventures, intelligence often enters the process through investigative market research and the analysis of economic trends.

At the top of the hierarchy stands intuitive trial and error. This is a level that works above cognitive trial and error because it adds an element of insight and personal experience

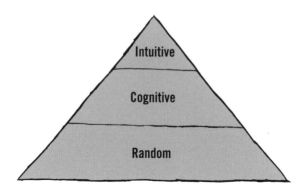

FIGURE 2-1: **The hierarchy of trial and error**

to the process. In addition to the intelligence gathered in processes of cognitive trial and error, insight realigns a venture to what is believed to be a more nearly correct direction. At this level of trial and error, both the linear and the holistic functions of the mind, the left brain and the right brain as it were, are guiding the trials with a view to create greater intuition, and reach a successful outcome faster and with greater accuracy.

Random trial and error

A good example of random trial and error is given by the father of Cybernetics, W. Ross Ashby. Cybernetics is the study of complex systems. Ashby's classic example of trial and error involves 1000 on/off switches that need to be set in one correct sequence.[1] For this type of random trial, he calculates the time required for a successful outcome based on the timing and process used to complete the trial. The assumption here is that neither intelligence nor intuition is of any value to the process. The only way to solve the problem is by random experimentation.

Another good example of random trial and error is an attempt to win a traditional lottery draw. Assuming that all numbers are chosen on a random basis, the choice of the lucky 6 or 7 numbers from the overall 39 to 49 numbers is based solely on chance. Depending on the timing and combination assumptions for such trials, success can be anticipated in terms of years or even centuries.

Brave entrepreneurs are those who best understand the value of random trial and error. Sometimes the greatest success factor for a venture is just showing up. Neither the amount of data available nor the level of personal insight at hand makes a significant difference in the outcome. In the gambling world, this is referred to as the workings of Lady Luck. No one knows when or how she will appear. By being in the game, you leave the door open for her. If you refuse to play, your door to success is closed and she will move on to the next address.

Though it may seem foolish to rely on luck to attain success, many good entrepreneurs understand that it is an inevitable part of success. An undertaking may have all the rational reasons to succeed but simply doesn't. Timing may be of the essence, and thus repeatedly attempting new ventures to allow random luck to strike may sometimes be the differentiating factor between success and failure.

René's trials and errors

A great example of a Canadian entrepreneur who understands the workings of chance is René Angélil. He is widely known as the husband and manager of the highly successful Canadian singer Céline Dion. What is less known is the story of how this venture began.

Angélil was an artist himself in the 50's and 60's. He began to work as one of the first professional managers in the Quebec music business in the 1970's. He had his first breakthrough managing the career of one of Quebec's most successful artists, Ginette Reno. In 1980, Reno abruptly ended a long and fruitful partnership with Angélil. Angélil was then left with nothing. During this difficult period, an acquaintance, bass player Michel Dion, gave him a tape of an unknown female singer. It turned out that the tape was to be Angélil's lucky lottery ticket.

It was only when he met the singer from the tape that he realized it was Michel Dion's 13 year-old sister, Céline. The girl obviously had no experience but she exuded a contagious will to succeed at a singing career. Angélil, a notable gambling man, decided to give her, and himself, a chance. In fact, he had very little to lose at the time. The rest of their multimillion dollar success story is a legend of the global entertainment industry. Their joint company, Les Productions Feelings, has grossed several hundred-million dollars over the last 20 years. However, it is interesting to remember that it all started with a lucky tape, good insight and the will to play against the odds.[2]

Luck and timing

Sometimes bad luck can turn into good luck. An accidental forest fire is often the first step in the rejuvenation of an entire ecosystem. As seen above, Angélil's will to take bigger risks came after his loss of his biggest source of income. Many Finnish success stories are also the result of difficult but right choices made after a spate of bad luck.

The Nokia Corporation was in a difficult situation in the early 1990's. It had made a catastrophic foray into the television manufacturing business and the losses almost bled the company into bankruptcy. The Swedish telecom corporation Ericsson even made a serious attempt to acquire Nokia during this period, but ultimately a deal couldn't be reached. The failure of the television manufacturing business helped encourage Nokia to abandon a sub-optimal diversification strategy and to focus on telecommunication and mobile phones.[3] This was perceived as a much riskier strategy at the time. In the case of Nokia, its relative bad luck turned out to be a driver for its later success. From the edge of bankruptcy some twenty years ago, Nokia emerged as one of the most valuable technology companies in the world. We discuss the Nokia story in more detail in Chapter 3.

Periods of difficulty often afford management the luxury of implementing bold moves. Of course, as we shall see in the next chapter, these decisions also involve a good deal of intelligence and hard work to produce successful outcomes. However, at this stage of our analysis, it is important to underline the unavoidable role of luck and good timing in producing positive outcomes.

At around the same period as Nokia's problems with television manufacturing, another large company was in dire straits. Faced with rising competition from Asian countries during the 1980's, the Finnish ship-building industry decided to consolidate itself. The Valmet ship-building unit, a state-owned company, was merged with Wärtsilä's ship-building operations. The resulting company, Wärtsilä Marine, was established in 1987. The merger proved to be a mistake. In 1989, the company filed the biggest bankruptcy in Finnish history. According to Martin Saarikangas, the President and CEO of Masa-Yards during the 1990's, the main reason for the bankruptcy was the drying up of the barter payment system between Finland and the Soviet Union, a system that had allowed the company to produce relatively low-quality, inefficient ships.[4]

This crisis was the basis for the acceptance of a bold new strategy to focus on high-end cruise ships produced for Carnival Cruises, the leading cruise operator of the Caribbean, by the company's successor, Masa-Yards.[5] In this case, as in the case of Nokia, the company's bad luck was one of the drivers for its bold turnaround.

One can even argue that Finland's worst luck ultimately turned into the initial spark of its good fortune. The period of the Second World War was extremely trying for the Finnish nation. This small country was caught in a power struggle between large nations, and bravely fought to maintain its independence. We cover this period of Finnish history in greater detail in Chapter 4's discussion of s*isu*. For our study of the Possibility Model, though, it is interesting to note that this devastating time in Finnish history laid some of the foundations for Finland's later success.

Finland had the misfortune of being hit with the Soviet Union's demands for large war reparations. However, the reparations forced Finns to build up a high-level industrial and academic infrastructure from practically nothing. They thereby provided the foundation for one of the Finnish miracles. Finland had to quickly integrate close to one million war veterans and Karelian refugees into its society and economy. The total population of Finland was around four million at that time. The industrial boom and massive gain in national wealth during the following decades are in part the result of the painful events related to the war, and to the pressure to rebuild the country and pay off the massive war debts.

Cognitive trial and error

The focus of cognitive trial and error is the production of facts and figures. Accurate and reliable data is the driver of trials, and is the motor behind the minimization of the risk of error. Examples of cognitive trial and error include market research, trend analysis, CRM analysis or the use of knowledge gathered from authoritative literature.

Efficient managers are masters of cognitive trial and error. They do their homework, they practice due diligence, they use research from within and outside their discipline before entering their ventures into commercial trials. To these managers, facts and data are all-important. Random elements of chance, or subjective elements coming from gut feelings, experience or personal intuition, are generally kept out of the process. In some ways, these managers like to mimic the rigors and objectivity of the scientific method.

Finnish managers and leaders usually excel at cognitive trial and error. Most business leaders in Finland have either an engineering or a business school background. Very few CEO's of large Finnish companies come from other academic backgrounds or have no academic backgrounds at all. High levels of education naturally incline managers to focus on facts and data as a basis for decision-making. Rationality is the prime motor of Finnish leadership. Processes and the impact of initiatives must be measurable and continuously assessed.

This has allowed for most Finnish companies to be at the cutting edge of scientific and industrial development on a global scale. At the height of its dominance of the mobile phone industry, Nokia's secret weapon was its ability to produce and distribute quality mobile phones using world-class technical and logistical processes.

As we saw in the previous chapter, Finland invests close to 4 percent of its GNP in research and development. It leads the world in the quality of its basic education. The country is number one in the PISA scores for 2003 and 2006. It was second in the world for the 2009 PISA national rankings, behind only South Korea. Finland is also a global leader in terms of patents awarded per capita.[6] On a yearly average, there are close to 36 patents awarded per one million Finns, as compared to less than one patent awarded per one million Americans.

This drive to experiment and excel in a wide range of sciences and technologies is at the source of the Finnish economic miracle of the past 60 years. It also explains the outstanding performance of many of the publicly listed companies on the Helsinki stock exchange. Nokia is clearly a case in point, but is only one significant part of a developed national ecosystem of high-performing technology companies. Kone, the Finnish elevator company, produces some of the world's most technologically advanced elevators. Elcoteq has a top reputation in mobile electronics. Orion is known for many of its prescription drugs. Arguably, Abloy produces the world's safest locking systems, and Ponsse makes the world's most advanced forest machines.

The list of Finnish companies with technological leadership in various segments of the economy is too long to reproduce here. It is enough to say that Finnish companies have led the way, in terms of scientific and technical experimentation, on a global scale in many industries. This makes Finland one of the world champions of cognitive trial and error.

Intuitive trial and error

Intuitive trial and error is at the top of the hierarchy because it includes the two lower levels and adds human experience and insight to the equation. Intuitive trial and error is important when developing products and services that represent a dramatic change in what exists at a given time. Focusing on what is already known or already exists will not give you a lasting competitive advantage. Focusing all of your attention on your current customers will not bring you to the next quantum leap in innovation.

The users of typewriters could not tell you that they wanted a personal computer. The demand for cell phones was not clear for most of the customers of land-line operators. These great innovations have come from the integration of all three levels of trial and error. With some luck, basic research and a vision of where the market is going, companies such as Microsoft, Nokia and Apple were able to create entirely new industries.

Examples of intuitive trial and error include reliance on personal experience, insight and belief in a personal vision. The application of this type of trial and error can draw the leadership of companies to make decisions that may, in some ways, contradict the results produced by objective or even scientific research. The initial market research prior to the launch of the Sony Walkman was inconclusive. The decision to launch the product despite the weak data proved to be the right one.

The invention of the text message by Finnish engineer Matti Makkonen was originally a stroke of luck or a by-product of other communication technology experiments. The addition of this feature to Nokia mobile phones was not intended to become a mainstream service. No research data was presented to support the future popularity of this feature. Yet twenty years and several billion messages later, text messaging is one of the revenue pillars of the global telecom industry.

Intuition's power to help us come up with correct insights is brilliantly presented in Malcolm Gladwell's popular book *Blink*.[7] One case that he writes about is the 7 million dollar purchase of a fake statue, the Kouros, by the highly reputable J. Paul Getty Museum in Malibu, California. The museum hired a team of scientists and lawyers for a period of 14 months to investigate the authenticity of the allegedly ancient artifact. The seller claimed that it was a genuine Greek statue from 600 BC.

The scientific examination was robust and concluded that the surface of the statue was covered with a thin layer of calcite which, in the scientists' opinion, proved the statue's very old age. Afterward, experienced ancient Greek art specialists immediately rejected the claim of authenticity after their first glance at the statue. It turned out that calcite can be created in months by the simple application of potato mold on the dolomite marble surface. In some cases the right experience leads to an insight that tells you, in the blink of an eye and much more than available objective facts, whether a venture is worthwhile.

Visionary leaders are masters of intuitive trial and error. They rely both on objective facts and figures and on personal experience and insight. They have a holistic approach to trial and error that integrates both parts of the mind and balances logic and intuition to attain the best possible outcome. These leaders are usually able to achieve higher levels of success because of the greater accuracy of the trials they launch and their ability to capture opportunities that have not yet revealed themselves.

In North America, the champions of trial and error become legends admired by all. From Thomas Edison to

Steve Jobs, the road to innovation and business success has often come after a long and risky series of challenging yet formative failures. For Thomas Edison, the formidable inventor, entrepreneur and father of the General Electric Company, errors and failures were the tools he used to correct and improve his inventions-in-the-making. His most famous invention, the electric light bulb, or in effect, the dramatic improvements that he brought to incandescent light, were the result of several thousand attempts. He always considered these failures small victories over the unknown as opposed to a discouraging series of defeats. Experience and insight comes more from error than success. He still holds the position of one of the most inventive entrepreneurs of all time, with 1093 patents to his name.[8]

For Steve Jobs, the road to the top of the global technology industry was long and eventful. Jobs co-founded Apple in 1977 with Steve Wozniak. Interestingly, one of the early investors and the company's second CEO was Mike Markkula, an American of Finnish descent. Jobs had a clear vision of the design and function of the computers the company needed to produce. He was one of the first to launch a series of commercially viable computers, the Apple II. He was also the first to see the potential of mouse-assisted graphical user interfaces.

Known to be uncompromising, Jobs had a falling out with Apple in 1984 and left the company. He moved on to a completely different business area, and this led him to Pixar studios, which was ultimately bought by the Disney Corporation. This transaction made him one of Disney's largest shareholders. Apple Computers grew steadily during the 80's and 90's. It catered to a loyal segment of the market but remained a marginal player compared to the likes of IBM and Microsoft at that time.

Jobs took charge of Apple again in 1997, and thirteen years later, in May 2010, Apple became the most valuable technology company in the world by surpassing the market capital value of Microsoft. In the summer of 2011 it even became, for a short time, the world's most valuable company altogether, exceeding the market value of Exxon with a market capitalization of 343 billion dollars. Jobs holds 230 patents either as primary inventor or as a co-inventor. He is credited with the huge successes of iTunes, the iPod, the iPhone and the iPad. In the end, it took Steve Jobs 33 years to beat out Microsoft and his friend Bill Gates. His trials and his errors are indeed legendary in the technology and media industries.[9]

Finland, like the rest of Europe, has had fewer high-profile champions of trial and error. There are, of course, enormously successful entrepreneurs on the European continent, but there are very few epic multibillionaire stories like those of Gates, Bezos or Jobs. European success stories generally follow a different scenario. It usually involves lower personal exposure to risk, and consequently a lower potential for personal reward.

Finland does have, however, its own visionary champions of trial and error. In addition to Nokia and its managers, who took impressive risks in the early 1990's, a few more solitary and impressive Finnish entrepreneurs deserve to be mentioned here. The Nokia story, and especially its fantastic turnaround of twenty years ago, will be dealt with in the following chapter on working harder and smarter. The tremendous success of the visionary Finnish gaming company Rovio and their unique blockbuster sensation, Angry Birds, will be covered in the final chapter, which discusses being yourself.

The story behind the security and anti-virus software company F-Secure and its founder Risto Siilasmaa is one of the most notable of the Finnish technology industry successes. In 1988, Siilasmaa established a software company called

Data Fellows. At the start, the company was doing programming in many different areas. In 1991, Siilasmaa wrote a book with Antti Hannula on the emerging importance of data security.

One of the early employees at Data Fellows, Ari Hyppönen, had an interest in the emerging phenomenon of computer viruses. He had written a book of his own on this subject as early as 1990. These books and their authors' insights led the company to continue significant IT development work in these areas despite the lack of customer demand during this period.

Very few people in the industry believed computer viruses to be a real problem. Siilasmaa recalls that at first many felt the company was producing the equivalent of anti-alien guns, weapons that could only be used to kill aliens. This is good if you believe in aliens, and indeed Data Fellows had the courage to believe in the coming of computer viruses as a major industry problem that would need to be solved.[10]

At that time, Finland had a lot of technical expertise in software development but very few professionals specialized in the software business. There was no venture funding available and no one who really understood the software licensing business. The company financed its R&D by bootstrapping and by offering computer usage courses on Macintosh. Because of all this, Siilasmaa admits that the company made several errors along the way.

Despite the general uncertainty, the company continued to study the problem and offer software solutions for it. One day, Siilasmaa remembers a fax dropping in with a serious information request for the company's anti-virus software. It was the first order in what would become a multibillion-dollar business. The spread of computer viruses over the Internet became a growing concern for consumers throughout the 1990's. Siilasmaa and his colleagues' early insight that there would be a need for developing a product and service that would keep viruses at bay became a reality.

Data Fellows grew quickly and in 1999, the company took on a new name: F-Secure. As resources were tight, no market research was involved in the early days of development. Advancement was mostly based on intuition about where the industry was going and what it would need to function efficiently in the future. Today, the company has a market capitalization of approximately 350 million Euros. Siilasmaa still owns 40 percent of the company and is a member of the board for the Nokia Corporation.

The Marimekko story is another fascinating Finnish tale of trial and error. Marimekko is one of the oldest and most successful Finnish textile and design companies. The company was co-founded in 1951 by fashion artist Riitta Immonen and the famous Finnish designer and printed-fabrics innovator Armi Ratia. The name Marimekko became synonymous with Finland's design identity in fashion and home interiors in the 60's and 70's. In the 80's, the company was bought by a large conglomerate, the Amer Corporation.

Amer was involved in many different businesses, including tobacco production and sporting goods. The new management began to bring mass production business practices to Marimekko. From the high-end consumer experience that it represented in its glory years, Marimekko implemented drastic changes to its corporate strategy. It now manufactured abroad, and started to cut corners and repel the high-level design talent of yesteryear. By the early 1990's it was on the verge of bankruptcy.

Kirsti Paakkanen, one of the most successful Finnish female entrepreneurs of her generation, had just sold her advertising agency to an international marketing company. She was settling into early retirement in southern France when she was offered the chance to jump in and save the struggling Marimekko. The turnaround was swift. Production was returned to Finland. Designers were empowered and put at the top of organizational charts. The renaissance of Marimekko had begun. To this day, Kirsti Paakkanen remains an icon of female entrepreneurship in Finland. Her travels along the ranges of trial and error, from leveraging good luck to implementing insights, are a legendary inspiration to many. We cover the story of Kirsti Paakkanen in greater detail in the last chapter.

Another Finnish success story worth mentioning is that of IObox. In the late 90's, the founder of IObox, Jari Ovaskainen, saw the growing need to create a mobile and web communication platform. He came up with a functional service for a personal e-mail exchange service in 1999 that quickly gathered 3 million users around the world. He made venture capital history in Finland by selling his company to the Spanish Teleoperator Telefonica for the stunning sum of 230 million Euros. This took place less than two years after IObox's creation.

One of the great challenges facing Finnish culture in generating future successes is its ability to experiment more with intuitive trial and error. A recurring weakness of Finnish corporate leadership is its systematic and sometimes sole dependence on facts and its over-rationalization of problems in the quest for solutions.[11] This feature of Finnish leadership is portrayed in the story on gut-feelings in the text-box below. To put it bluntly, Finnish problem-solving culture is often stuck at the level of cognitive trial and error. Though the Finnish mastery of this level of trial and error has contributed and continues to contribute to its tremendous success, one can still argue that Finns are sometimes too "smart" for their own good. They often have difficulties in trusting themselves and their intuition, which in many cases could provide the lever needed for a higher level of innovation and growth.

No gut feelings, please. We're Finnish.

A young Finnish executive, Sari Saarinen, is preparing for her big presentation to the company's board of directors. She glances at her PowerPoint presentation just before being called into the board room. The room is filled with well-respected and established figures of Finnish industry and business. She manages to hide her feeling of slight intimidation behind cool and collected body language and fairly frozen facial expressions.

The chairman nods to her: "Begin, please." She drives her proposal through a long icy patch of corporate silence and the stony expressions of the 11 members of the board of directors. She goes through the market trends, and highlights the few elements of research that support her position. At the end of her presentation she formalizes her decision proposal to the board for a significant investment in this new product and service.

The board members take a few long seconds to reshuffle their papers. The chairman asks the first question: "Is that it?" "Yes, that's it," Sari replies with a slight stutter, adding: "Was something missing?" The chairman asks: "Well, how do you know for sure that this venture will be a success in Finland?" She answers: "Well, it is part of a clear and growing trend in many European countries, including countries that are close to us, like Sweden."

Another board member breaks in, with a hint of annoyance and nationalist reproach: "Are you saying that Finns are like every other European country?" Sari gropes for a proper reply: "Well, no… I mean yes, sir. Our focus groups in Finland as well as our market research among our current customers is positive." The chairman cuts her off impatiently: "But how do you truly know that the rest of the 5 million Finns are going to be interested in this?" Sari stiffens and says: "Well, based on this initial data, I have a very good gut feeling that this will be big here too." Another board member with a banking background takes the floor, saying: "What was that? A gut feeling? My dear young lady, nobody in this country makes an investment of this size on a gut feeling!"

The chairman shakes his head and says: "I can tell you what I see here. I see that this is a dying business in traditional retail, and my own gut feeling, I'm afraid, is that you have too little data here." Sari tries to rescue the situation: "But sir, this is the Internet and it is quite a different story...." The chairman is unimpressed. "Oh, don't start that again. The Internet hasn't changed the fundamentals. Facts are facts. When you have more facts to present us, then we shall be ready to make a decision. Thank you." And that is the end of her presentation.

The young executive leaves the board room with the strange sensation of waking up from a bad dream. She later conducts a more significant amount of research and the results continue to speak in favor of her new service. Following the service's much-delayed launch, it turns out that even her most optimistic income forecasts were way short of the mark. The sales from this new service are, in the end, three times her original forecast for the first year of operations.

Some Finnish paradoxes

Popular yet scary

The global benchmark figures tell an interesting story about Finnish entrepreneurship. According to the Global Entrepreneurship Index (GEI),[12] Finland is at the bottom of the Western world's scale for high-growth entrepreneurship. According to this study only 0.3 percent of the population of Finland has aspirations toward high-growth entrepreneurship. This figure is five times lower than the figures seen in countries such as the USA or even Iceland. It represents two times fewer potential entrepreneurs than even the neighboring countries of Norway or Sweden. The paradox comes with the reading of another figure of the GEI: Finns have an above-average positive attitude towards entrepreneurship. In most other countries, a positive attitude towards entrepreneurship usually correlates with a higher amount of entrepreneurial activity.

In his insightful paper on this issue,[13] Professor Erkko Autio proposes some elements of an explanation for this paradox. He identifies history, absorption of talent by the larger corporations and culture as potential explicative factors. Unlike the USA or even Sweden, Finland has a very short history of entrepreneurship. There are very few role models for this kind of activity and very few experienced managers available with an entrepreneurial background. It is also the case that the traditional industries and large technology companies have succeeded in hiring and keeping a large share of the talented entrepreneurial people available in the country. This has allowed many of the big technology and engineering companies to grow and prosper. Nokia, again, is a good case in point as it has probably been chiefly responsible for capturing much of the local entrepreneurial talent in the high-growth technology sector.

On the issue of the lack of entrepreneurial culture, it is more difficult to speculate. It is, however, interesting to note that while Finland is at the bottom of the GEI, it is in relatively good company there. Other countries with low incidences of small, high-growth entrepreneurial companies are Japan and France. It is maybe the nature of collectivist or

FIGURE 2-2:
The impact of Amara's law on growth

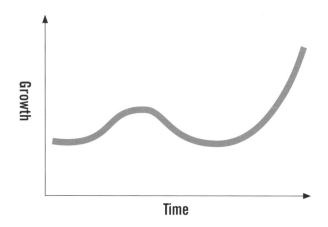

socialist-driven societies to channel entrepreneurial activity in a different way than more individualistic societies such as the United States. Finland's general egalitarianism naturally affects the way it will organize its innovation efforts.

Though most Finns now share a positive view of those who are engaged in small, high-growth entrepreneurship, many of them still seem to feel it is unnatural and unduly risky to try to create something great and new from the work of a handful of innovators with a vision. It is also interesting to note that only one quarter of entrepreneurs in Finland are women.[14] Though the country's universities produce a roughly equal number of male and female professionals, there are clearly fewer female entrepreneurs. This may be explained by a series of social and cultural factors, but it is an obvious area of potential growth for the future.

It may also be that Finns are more rational and well-informed about the risks involved in starting their own ventures. Much like the stock exchange, technology ventures often evolve on a boom and bust continuum. In the technology industry, we find that growth is greatly affected by Amara's Law.[15] According to this law, the market tends to overestimate the impact of growth in the short term and underestimate its impact in the long term. Figure 2-2 gives a picture of the S-shaped progression of growth impacted by Amara's Law. It follows that financial success or ruin in this area is as much a question of timing as it is a question of raw talent. For Jari Ovaskainen, the successful exit from the startup IObox occurred literally two months before the burst of the Internet bubble.

Can't win and can't fail

According to the former CEO of MySQL, the well-known Finnish entrepreneur Mårten Mickos, Finland is a country where it is both forbidden to succeed and forbidden to fail.[16] By saying this, he refers to a nation that bypasses excellence because of a culturally based fear of failure as well as a surprising fear of success. He claims that Finns tend to pity those who fail and envy those who succeed to a point where neither is a desired outcome for anyone who is either too fearful or too smart to engage in a risky business venture.

For some of those prominent Finns interviewed for this book, Finnish social jealousy is indeed a genuine challenge in the culture. You cannot speak of your success without triggering some negative feelings of envy at least in some part of the population. This kind of social reclusion of the successful creates a dearth of positive role models to inspire others. The low profile of successful entrepreneurs turns into low levels of interest in entrepreneurial activity from potential high-growth entrepreneurs. Finland, as we have seen, is a young and highly egalitarian country. It may well be that most people do not know how to react towards the emergence of a new group of wealthy and successful people.

Mårten Mickos, prior to his great success at MySQL, founded one of the notable flops of Finnish start-up history, MatchOn Sports, which lost close to seven million Euros of invested capital. Mickos, a native Finn, still remembers how this experience exposed him to the national stigma against failure. In Silicon Valley, thankfully, the experience was seen as good preparation for his ultimate success at MySQL. At over one billion Euros, MySQL is the most successful start-up exit in Finland to date. Because of the challenging cultural landscape, many talented Finns and would-be-entrepreneurs prefer to share the risk of ventures within a corporation that can withstand the fluctuations in the market and also keep their anonymity behind a facilitating corporate veil.

Afraid not to be right

The Finnish relationship to error can also partly explain the relatively subdued entrepreneurial culture in Finland. As we have seen in earlier chapters, Finns pride themselves on their level of education. Finns are dedicated to getting things "right." Literacy, mathematics and natural sciences all require the ability to produce objective answers. In this learning culture, errors are frowned upon, and thus many who can't muster the courage find refuge in silence or inaction. High PISA scores are not given for high entrepreneurial skills and an ability to tolerate and manage risk. The phrase "Finland teaches you a lesson" has now become one of the catch phrases that the new national brand strategy referred to earlier. Admitting that we do not know all the answers, or that no amount of reading or counting will help get to those answers, can be a discomforting thought for many Finns.

In some ways, this uneasy relationship to error is similarly instilled in Japanese youth. As a young teacher in Japan, I noticed that while I was correcting the papers of my talented students in their presence, they would twitch a part of their body or physically tense up at each one of my correcting strokes on their work. This body language would sometimes be accompanied by a verbal tic: "Sorry, sorry teacher." This relationship to error is not as extreme in Finland, but it shares some similarities to the Japanese culture in this respect. The fear or the shame surrounding error is a great driver of success. Most Finns and Japanese would work fiercely to learn a lesson now and avoid the embarrassment of being taught a lesson later. However, this cultural feature is also an inhibiting factor in the pursuit of success, especially when navigating in the realm of the unknown.

This is why both errors and successes that would otherwise be visible in error-tolerant cultures such as one finds in North America are often hidden in Finland. In my 20 years of experience in higher-education and various executive roles in Finnish companies, I have repeatedly noticed that errors must be dealt with carefully and privately. Special attention to hiding or diminishing the significance of errors committed by your peers is one of the unwritten rules of Finnish working life. This is not a question of lack of honesty. It is a question of courtesy and respect, of being kind to the one who errs. However, it reinforces a potentially damaging relationship to errors because they are left to create undue personal stress and are not communicated to a wider audience who might benefit from them. The current Minister for European Affairs and Foreign Trade, Alexander Stubb, also raised the greater acceptance of failures as one of the key challenges facing Finnish entrepreneurs in the future.[17]

In this respect, more literature on business failures would be welcome in Finland. In one extremely interesting book on the largest business failures of the past 25 years,[18] many of the greatest errors in business history are dissected for the benefit of future generations, such as Kodak's huge blunder around the coming of digital photography, and the multibillion-dollar flop of Motorola's Iridium world phone. Needless to say, a book such as this would have serious difficulties being published in Finland. This is mostly because of the culture of secrecy and relative shame that exists around error in the Finnish culture.

There have been some impressive corporate errors committed in Finland. One of the biggest corporate errors to become publicly known was the purchase by the state-owned operator Sonera of the German UMTS licenses in 2000. Two years later, the company had to write off 4.3 billion Euros from the corporate balance sheet, which made the purchase of the licenses worthless. This was a big blow to the national ego.

The CEO at the time, Kaj-Erik Relander, became a publicly disliked figure. He moved to London to join a venture capital firm. In 2004 he became the target of a criminal action, instigated by an anonymous journal which purported to reveal the strange and allegedly illegal goings-on at Sonera during his term as CEO. After a witch-hunt media extravaganza, he and some other former directors of the company served suspended prison sentences for having violated employee privacy rights. It seems that the Finnish taxpayers were not alone in their dislike of Mr. Relander's errors. At least, though, these errors were well-documented, and should therefore serve as a warning to stakeholders faced with similar challenges in the future.

One very concrete public Finnish error which turned out to serve as a preventive lesson is the economic crisis of the early 1990's. After a long period of economic growth in the

1980's, Finland was surprised by the economic downturn caused mainly by the dissolution of the Soviet Union and the special protocol of trade between the two countries. Much of the rapid growth in Finland had been financed by foreign loans. Unfortunately for many, the Finnish currency was devalued and many of the Finnish banks needed to be bailed out by the government.

Since then, mechanisms have been put in place to control the risk exposure of Finnish banks. This reform turned out to be one of the reasons why Finland handled the economic crisis of 2009 better than most other European countries. In the light of what has happened over the past two years in Iceland, Greece and Ireland, Finns can consider themselves lucky to have erred almost twenty years earlier and learned from their mistakes.

2.2 Olympic trials and tribulations

The Olympic history of Finland presents several stories of interest in the study of success. For starters, Finland is one of the most successful nations in the world in the Olympics if you measure medals won *per capita*. Finland comes in third, after only the former East Germany and Norway in the world *per capita* medal rankings.

During the 1920's, in the early days of its freshly obtained independence, Finland became known as a country of fantastic runners such as Hannes Kolehmainen, Ville Ritola and Paavo Nurmi. The most famous of these athletes was Nurmi, who was also one of the most successful runners of all time. Although his record of nine Olympic gold medals, won from 1920 to 1928, was matched 68 years later by the American Carl Lewis, Nurmi still holds the record for total Olympic medals (12) in track and field.

Finnish Olympic trials

The recipe for success in competitive sports is perhaps more dependent on hard work and courage than on the astute applications of trial and error processes. The next two chapters of this book dealing with work and *sisu* shall therefore provide some more examples of Finnish sports achievements. However, the hosting of Olympic and large-scale events in Finland also presents an excellent case study of the intricacies of trial and error. Because of my personal involvement in these interesting ventures, I recount the stories as I have experienced them, in an effort to share what I have learned from our Olympic trials and errors.

As a young republic, Finland was eager to appear on the world stage. It felt that its new status as a nation needed to be reinforced by internationally visible activity and luster. In sports, this meant the Olympic Games. Following its accession to nationhood in 1917, Finland was represented by stellar athletes throughout the 1920's. In fact, at the Olympic Games of 1924 in Paris, Finland finished second only to the United States in the medal rankings, ahead of France and the United Kingdom, which came in third and fourth respectively. On its own scale, this is another Finnish miracle.

The young Finnish state of the 1930's coveted an even greater prize to reinforce its place among nations: the hosting of the Olympic Games. Its first attempt came during the 1930's, and its bold candidature was rewarded by the International Olympic Committee's decision to have Helsinki host the 1940 Summer Olympic Games. Unfortunately for Finland, these games were cancelled as most of the world was at war, and Finland was still recovering from the Winter War of 1939 with the Soviet Union. This was a case of trial and error failing in the end because of exceptional bad luck.

Finns were persistent in their efforts to host the Olympic Games. Following the first post-war Olympics Games of London in 1948, they again obtained the right to organize the Olympic Games of 1952. In this respect, the country's inability to host the 1940 Olympic Games was the basis for its successful campaign for the 1952 Games. One must remember that Finland was only eight years earlier a country fairly devastated by its wars against the Soviet Union. To make things more difficult, Finland was hit with demands from the Soviets for huge war reparations. The last payments of the war debt were actually made only a few weeks before the opening ceremony of the 1952 Helsinki Olympics.

When the torch was lit by the retired running legend Paavo Nurmi, Finns experienced more than the opening of a great sports event. For most Finns, it was a symbol of victory over adversity, winning against the odds, and a display of durable statehood performed on the world stage. The 1952 Helsinki Games were a great success. For many political observers they were also seen as the last true Olympic Games because most of the subsequent games were boycotted by smaller or larger groups of states for political reasons.

For most of the post-war period, Finland continued to produce high-level Olympic athletes. In particular, Finland, along with its Nordic neighbors, dominated cross-country skiing events at many of the winter games of the 1960's, 1970's and 1980's. Juha Mieto and Marja-Liisa Kirvesniemi are among the Finnish sporting legends of these disciplines. Their successes, and Finland's rapid development as a nation, fuelled Finland's desire to host the Winter Olympics. Until the mid-1990's, Finland had made an impressive four attempts to host the winter games. All of them failed, partly due to the absence of high enough mountains to host the alpine skiing events, which have traditionally been the crown jewel of the Winter Olympics.

In the mid-1990's, the International Olympic Committee made an amendment to the Olympic Charter that would allow countries such as Finland, which, for geographic reasons, could not host the winter games, to present a joint bid with a neighboring nation. In many Olympic circles this was called the Finnish rule, since it almost seemed to be made for Finland's special circumstances. In view of the change in the IOC Charter, the Finnish National Olympic Committee formally posed its candidacy in early 1998 for the Winter Games of 2006. Interestingly enough, Finland was not alone in testing the new Olympic rule. The candidacy of Klagenfurt, from Austria, included proposed cooperation with two neighboring countries: Italy and Slovenia.

Olympic errors and victories: a personal view

I vividly remember how I was recruited into this 1998 campaign to host the Winter Games. At that time, I had six years of experience in international sports relations under my belt. As the Secretary General of an influential international sport science organizations, ICSSPE, I had been in weekly contact with the International Olympic Committee. I knew the organization well, especially its leader, Juan Antonio Samaranch, who had taken under his wing both me and my then-boss, Professor Paavo Komi, the President of ICSSPE.[19]

Paavo Komi is actually the common answer I give to the inevitable question that Finns ask when they meet a foreigner for the first time: "Why did you come to Finland?" Many Finns, who sometimes fail to recognize their country's strengths, wonder why anyone would actually choose to immigrate to their country. Thus the tone of this question is often delivered with a suspicious twist. If you didn't come for a woman, then they must have thrown you out of Canada! For these Finns, Finland is far from being a miracle. The miracle, in their eyes, is perhaps the fact that some people, even from the wealthiest parts of the world, would find their way here of their own free will.

My standard and truthful answer to this amusingly repetitive Finnish question is: "A phone call." I continue by telling them that as my lack of luck would have it, it wasn't a beautiful blond maiden taken straight from an Elovena Finnish-porridge advertisement who called me. It was a balding male senior scientist offering me a highly international job.

Professor Paavo Komi is the person who gave me that call. He was one of the leading biomechanists in the world. NASA even sought his advice on physiological issues dealing with re-entry to the earth's atmosphere. Paavo Komi is a living example of the systematic efforts of Finland to make investments in higher education and top level research after the Second World War. He was one of many Finns and Europeans who went to do their post-doctoral studies in the United States as early as the 1950's and 1960's. Due to his long and meritorious career, he was elected to the presidency of ICSSPE, and he hired me as his Secretary General.

So right after writing my New York bar exams and dreaming of a career on Wall Street, I ended up on "little shop street (Kauppakatu)" in Jyväskylä, in Central Finland. Some of my less inspired Finnish colleagues have listened to this story and said: "Sorry, André. Shit happens!" Though this may be amusing from one perspective, my decision was, in fact, a serious attempt to take the road less travelled by, my own attempt at exercising intuitive trial and error, and it led directly to my discovery of the Finnish miracle.

Six years later, an occurrence of random luck hit me in the form of another fateful phone call. The call I received was from a Finnish industrial icon of the time: Martin Saarikangas. He was the CEO of Masa-Yards, the shipbuilding yards of Finland. At the time, the Masa-Yards were responsible for the construction of half of the world's Carnival Cruise ships. Some of these mega-ships are like cities on water, costing up to 700 million Euros to build. Martin Saarikangas, or Masa as many called him, was also the chairman of the Finnish Ice Hockey Federation and, early in the 90's, a much-discussed potential candidate for the presidency of Finland.

Masa was in some respects a caricature of what Finns call a *patruuna*, i.e., a distinguished old-school Finnish business leader. He was deadly direct and somewhat harsh in his communication style. Given my role in international sports and his role in Finnish ice hockey, our paths had crossed and we had become "nodding acquaintances." This is common in Finland between business people who vaguely know each other. As they cross each other, there is no wasted speech; just a grunted "Hei" for "Hello" or a silent nod will do to acknowledge someone's presence.

I will always remember that first phone call from Masa. "Hello, this is Martin Saarikangas speaking," he said, and then went straight to the point: "What are you doing nowadays?" "Well, I'm doing an MBA, and I…" "Ok, so you will stop that and come work for us." "Ok, but…" I said, thinking to myself that he was displaying, at least for me, an exotic leadership approach. "So what is it that *we* are going to do?" "*We* are going to get the Winter Olympics for Finland. Be at my office at 08:00 tomorrow morning." That was the gist of my job interview, and off I went on a one-and-a-half year adventure to make Finland's Olympic dream come true.

My role would be that of the marketing director – read "lobbyist" – of the Helsinki 2006 Winter Olympic Games candidacy. Of course, like most Finnish employers, Masa had done his homework on me, and hiring a foreigner in such a nationally sensitive position was not an easy choice. In Finland, your reputation is the most valuable asset you have. Trust is the social and economic fluid that makes things work so efficiently in Finland. We look at the power of trust generally, and its special role in the Finnish success story, in the next chapter.

The 2006 Helsinki Winter Olympic Candidate City team was fairly small. The CEO was Jari Piirainen, the former general director of the Finnish Ski Federation. A large man with a big heart, he is a good communicator and an expert on Olympic winter sports, especially skiing. He was the ideal leader of the operational team. We also had one of the two Finnish members of the International Olympic Committee, Pirjo Häggman, working with us. She was the first woman ever elected to the IOC and was very much liked by most of her IOC colleagues. She is an infectiously cheerful person with an unbelievably loud voice. This probably comes from her profession as an adamant teacher of physical education.

Both Jari and Pirjo would face difficulties later in their careers but both were and still are, in my book, great individuals. Together with three talented young ladies fresh out of business school, we were the core operational team of the Finnish bid. This was indeed a micro-team in comparison with the extensive teams of the cities of Sion and Turin, with staff and budgets over three times greater than our own. However, for a small country such as Finland, the three million Euros of campaign money awarded by the state and the City of Helsinki was a financial stretch. It was still clearly below the international average for this type of campaign: the Sion and Turin budgets were each in the 10 million Euros range. Finland did, however, guarantee the Helsinki games, with a national parliamentary guarantee package of a whopping half-a-billion Euros. This extensive governmental support is unheard-of for any other event in the world.

Despite the challenges, our bid was doing well. We had the sympathy and respect of many members of the IOC. They appreciated the Olympic heritage of Finland as well as the reputation of Finland as a modern and technologically advanced country.

In the course of the bid, I got to know many high-profile Finns. This gave me a new perspective on Finland and opened my mind to some of the strong cultural features of the country. There is something about each country's pool of celebrities that offers powerful insights into the soul of a nation and its culture. In many ways, the well-known personalities of each country reflect some elements of the rest of its people.

In the case of Masa Saarikangas, I was exposed to highly efficient yet sometimes brutal leadership styles typical of old-guard Finnish leaders. We were not on the best of terms at first. His way of ordering people about and creating fear around him was maybe good for pumping world-class ships out of shipping yards, but it was not always conducive to making the desired impression on our sophisticated international voters. He needed me and others for this. His way of communicating, in all languages, needed some tweaking.

Like some other Finnish executives I know, Masa liked to give his collaborators nicknames. For our two IOC members it was *Purjo* and *Piötr* for Pirjo and Peter. Not the most flattering names since they respectively refer to a vegetable (leek) and an undesired "Russification" of a first name, but everyone took it with a smile. In my case, I was re-baptised "Chakal" which he thought was hysterically close to my surname: Chaker. He would love to say "Chakal, do this" and "Chakal, do that..."

At one point it naturally started to get on my nerves. I could enjoy amusing name-calling as long as it went both ways and was conducive to building a good team spirit. In this case, nobody dared to play trial and error with Masa and call him anything other than his self-approved nickname

"Masa" for "Martin." I therefore took a risk in slightly breaking this Finnish fear-of-authority syndrome.

At a meeting of the Executive Board of the IOC in South Korea, where I was able to chat privately and actively with several old IOC acquaintances, I was once again asked by Masa to give a report over lunch to a large delegation of Finnish representatives. "Chakal, tell them" was my usual cue, but for this particular report I decided to use some of my basic college acting skills. I shot myself up like a sleeping soldier from his barracks' bed and shouted "*Oui, mon Général Hannibal!*"

I was suddenly surrounded by deep Finnish silence. Some of our younger team members had only an expression of shock and fear on their faces. Everyone must have thought that I was going home in a bag. Masa looked at me with his emotionless Viking face and after a few long seconds exposed his pirate teeth in uncontrolled laughter. "Ha, Ha, Hannibal. Général Hannibal. That suits me very well!" From that point onwards we became good friends. Hannibal and Chakal were a force to be reckoned with in international sports lobbying.

Another great Finn I met during the Olympic bid was Ere Kokkonen. Ere was a celebrated film director and script writer. He is the creator of the Uno Turhapuro films, which are in some ways the Finnish equivalents of the Monty Python films. The secret of Ere Kokkonen was his creativity and touching authenticity. This success driver is covered in the last chapter of the book, but since Ere's role in the Olympic Bid was so important, I mention him already here.

Ere was charged with the task of preparing the film of the Finnish bid for the final presentation in South Korea. I worked with him on the specifications for the clip and gave him feedback on his script. When it came time to choose the two main characters for the film, I was encouraged to audition for the part. After practicing some intuitive trial and error, things went my way. For the price of a marketing director, the bid got itself, some say, a decent actor and presenter for our official film. To be honest, I was surprised but pleased to be selected for the part. I was paired with the talented Anna Sorainen, who did a splendid job in presenting the Helsinki bid to the world.

If Masa was one of the tallest Finns I had ever met at well over two meters, then Ere was certainly the shortest at less than 160 centimeters. Ere is a legend of Finnish film and entertainment. As the Yoda of Finnish cinematography, he was a master at making Finns laugh. He was also an extremely warm and intelligent man. His limited English skills left him without an international career, but his work in Finnish film and theater shall never be forgotten. Regrettably, he passed away in 2008.

I remember flying via Zurich to Montreal for Christmas vacation in 1998. I was especially pleased with the main title of the day's "Tribune de Genève," which read: *"Le Grand Danger c'est Helsinki!"* This referred to the perceived lead the Swiss media believed we had over Sion and Turin. Upon my return to the office in early January, I showed the paper to my teammates, who were also full of satisfaction with our projected image.

At the same time, an important fax rolled into the office to the laughing ignorance of the just-returned-from-vacation team. Minutes later, the phone rang. It was a reporter from the *New York Times* asking for our colleague Pirjo Häggman. Abandoning her usual broad smile, she became stonily serious. "What do you intend to respond to the accusation letter you have received from the IOC President?" the *Times* reporter asked. "What letter? I don't know what you are talking about."

She hung up and ran to the fax machine. It was a letter from IOC President Samaranch asking her to explain why her ex-husband, Bjarne Häggman, had received over 20 000 dollars in "consulting fees" from the Salt Lake City bid. She was devastated. She said she knew nothing of Bjarne's dealings, especially after their divorce. We colleagues believed her, but the Finnish media did not. Finns, who are widely recognized as one of the least corrupt nations on Earth, have very little tolerance for even the appearance of the self-serving pocketing of personal benefits. It was the beginning of the end of her career at the IOC and the beginning of our intensified struggle to keep our bid going.

Our main challenge wasn't just that our own IOC member had to resign. It was the IOC member visiting ban on all candidate cities that made it extremely difficult to sell our plan and our country. With less than seven months to go, we made a brave attempt to make our case to the IOC. Much would depend on the final presentation and the time we would have in Seoul, Korea prior to the vote. Despite our best efforts, the games went to Turin. But for someone who has always believed in the virtues of trial and error, I had a gut feeling that Finland would get another chance to prove itself on the battleground of world-class athletic events.

The Nairobi trial

"Have a nice trip to Nairobi, André, but I think you have little chance of succeeding." It was with these encouraging words that my former boss, the big Masa, left me before our lobbying trip to Nairobi.

He was right. The odds were not at all in our favor. It was in December 2001 that I received a phone call from Antti Pihlakoski, the CEO of Finnish Athletics, asking me to assist the athletics federation in getting the World Championships in Athletics to Helsinki for 2005. He and his high profile team of Finnish politicians, such as former minister Ilkka

Kanerva and former Prime Minister Harri Holkeri, were serious about bringing this massive event to Finland.

Over the phone I asked Antti, "Who do you think we'll be up against?" "Oh just a few European cities. Maybe Berlin, Rome, Moscow, Brussels and Budapest." "Well, it will be a piece of cake then!" I said sarcastically. "And this would be the second time for Finland, wouldn't it?" I asked. "Yes, we organized the first World Championships in 1983," confirmed Antti.

With that kind of competition, most international experts in sports politics would tell you that this was an impossible venture. Under any rational exercise of cognitive trial and error, this was going to be a very challenging case. First, a city of barely one million inhabitants faces off against some of the biggest, wealthiest and most prestigious cities in Europe and in the world. This is more than a David and Goliath story. It is a David against five Goliaths story. And then this small city and country had already been awarded the event at its inception in 1983. With over 200 other nations eligible to host the event – and maybe 30 countries with the kind of resources to really pull it off – one would have been completely justified in saying that it was outright impossible for Finland to win the right to host it once again.

In international sporting events terms, it simply wasn't Finland's "turn." However, underneath the surface was a potential that very few saw. I immediately felt that the leadership of Finland's athletics federation had some special insight on the matter, and I was thus ready to embark on a process of intuitive trial and error with them. "Ok, Antti, count me in," I said. "If you're crazy enough to try, I'm crazy enough to join you."

The circumstances leading up to the selection of the 2005 organizers were exceptional in a few respects. The main stage-setting element of the competition was that with only three-and-a-half years to go, the city of London had pulled out of its responsibility to host these championships. With such little time remaining, the international federation was re-organizing a crisis-like bidding process to find a new host for the event.

This important aspect of the process became our biggest opportunity. The International Association of Athletics Federations (IAAF) was in trouble and therefore perhaps more willing to consider cities and countries that had staged the event before and ignore the unwritten every-city-should-have-a-turn rule. In addition, the London pull-out had just demonstrated that a large city was as risky as it was attractive. Finally, a short bidding process always favors smaller cities and countries.

When I met some old opponents of the Olympic bid from the Italian and Roman camp who had been part of the Turin victory over Helsinki for the Winter Olympics, they commented on the bidding process by saying: "In five months, the only thing you can organize in Italy is chaos!" To which I smiled and confidently answered in Italian "*Sì lo so, e per questa raggione oggi guadagneremo*," which means "Yes, I know, and for that reason today we are going to win." Both the language skills and the cockiness come courtesy of my Italian grandmother.

We were sure that our appeal to the rational side of the IAAF Council members was sound. We had a solid bid with strong circumstantial factors favoring a cautious return to Helsinki. However, we pondered long and hard on how we could win the hearts of the Council members. After all, we make most of our decisions in life more with our hearts than with our minds. In our address to the Council, we had to cook up something irrationally appealing that would tip the balance in our favor. It had to be bold and it had to be authentic.

"*Niin minä neitonen sinulle laulan kuin omalle kullalleeni*" (In this way, young lady, I sing to you as if you were my own sweetheart). These were the first words of our presentation to the IAAF Board. They were, surprisingly, sung aloud and sung in Finnish. I was the lucky team member to sing part of this old Finnish folk song to start our presentation to the IAAF Council.

The predominantly dark eyes of the 27 Council Members were stupefied. They must have asked themselves, "What has the Helsinki team been drinking today? It must be strong stuff! They are the last of the six cities to present, and they only have 40 minutes to state their case. And here they are having a foreign-looking Finn sing folk tunes to us in Finnish! Those Finns are crazy." If those were the thoughts we provoked in the minds of the Council, then it definitely had the intended effect. Rule number one in business communications: the attention grabber, the presentation ice breaker, is the key to introducing the message and setting the tone for the presentation.

Behind me was a large black-and-white photograph of an elegant black athlete jumping in the air. It was a picture of the great triple jumper Ferrera da Silva from Brazil. Both Finland and Ferrera reached a critical climax during the same period in history. Ferrera was one of the stars of the 1952 Olympic Games in Helsinki. Ferrera won gold and Finland won international recognition right after its two harsh wars against the Soviet Union. Ferrera is said to have sung, in Finnish, the same folk song we used in Nairobi, to the delight of many Finnish ladies at the time of the Helsinki games of 1952.

An even more touching part of the story is that almost fifty years later Ferrera da Silva sang this song during a visit to Helsinki just prior to the Olympic Games in Sydney in the year 2000. To the surprise of many, this fairly frail old man from Brazil started to sing the song, in Finnish, to the members of the Finnish national team. His voice was saying, "I remember the spirit of Helsinki of 1952. May the same spirit be with you in Sydney." It is interesting to note here that the Finnish athlete Arsi Harju won gold in the shotput in Sydney. Maybe Ferrera's old song was more helpful than some might think...

In Nairobi, Peter Tallberg, the IOC member for Finland, and Tapani Ilkka, the then-President of the National Olympic Committee, got up and started circulating authentic commemorative medals of the 1952 games. The elders of the IAAF Council were delighted. I explained the gesture: "These medals are symbols of the spirit of Helsinki and the spirit of athletics that Ferrera was singing about. We may not have everything that bigger cities have, but we have the heart of athletics in our city, and this heart creates memories for a lifetime."

These words seemed to touch our decision-makers but it was the Brazilian representative to the IAAF board, Augusto De Melo, a charming man with a strong Brazilian accent, who drove the point home in the question-and-answer session following our presentation: "I would like to thank you for remembering our great national hero, Ferrera da Silva. As you know, Ferrera died last year, but I know that if he were here today, he would certainly vote for Helsinki. Thank you." One down, twenty-six Council members to go. The battle for the hearts and minds of the IAAF Council was on.

We had an impressive group in Nairobi. I had the great pleasure of presenting them to the Council, in English and in French. Harri Holkeri, a former prime minister of Finland with a strong reputation as an international peacemaker, was and is a man of stature, an old-school politician with a commanding aura of respect and credibility. Ilkka Kanerva, the consummate veteran of Finnish politics, was at that time a former minister and the current deputy speaker of the house. He later became Finland's Minister of Foreign Affairs. Ilkka is an authentic sports lover with tremendous social skills. Suvi Lindén, a rising star in Finnish politics, was Minister of Culture at the time and later Minister of Transport and Communication. Lindén was perceived as an elegant platinum-blond politician who made a solid impression among the team of predominantly male dark suits before us.

Antti Pihlakoski and Mikko Vanni are the Batman and Robin of Finnish athletics. They were the architects of the bid and the motor behind our belief that the impossible was possible. They are consummate Finnish entrepreneurs who have mastered the art of intuitive trial and error. Finally our team was blessed by the legend of Finnish and global athletics himself, the great Lasse Virén. Lasse's humility is a trademark of Finnish manners and of the Finnish communication style. Totally unassuming, this amazing athlete is the one who ran that incredible race in Munich in 1972 by falling at the beginning of the 10 000 meters and still coming out victorious.

Lasse was our last speaker. We thought about this carefully in our rehearsals and we simply advised him to speak to his colleagues from the heart and to just be himself. He told them in a few sentences in simple English that the young Lasse Virén ran himself to exhaustion in the mountains of Kenya, and that the older Lasse Virén just wanted to see his old friends again in Helsinki in 2005. That was truly a Finnish moment: a few genuine words that mean a lot.

"And the organizers of the 10th World Championships in Athletics will be…" Lamine Diack, the patriarch of world athletics, opened the envelope and disclosed its contents. No one from the Finnish media was present: no TV, no print, no radio. Even the Finnish ambassador to Kenya was back in Finland at the time. But thank God for CNN! They are everywhere

all the time. "Helsinki!" shouted Diack, and thirteen crazy Finns jumped in the air. I was delirious with joy. My God! We can actually win these things! There *is* a God!

I called my girlfriend Hanna (now my wife) and told her I loved her, I loved life and everything was now just perfect. At the ambassador's residence, without the ambassador, we had an unbelievable party in the plus-30-degrees African heat, and despite this we of course went to the Finnish sauna. I remember singing *"Me ollaan sankareita kaikki"*[20] naked in the swimming pool with Lasse Virén. A triumph *à la Finlandaise* that I have not quite experienced since.

CHAPTER 3
Working harder and smarter

> One should work as if one will live
> eternally, and should have the spirit of
> one who will die within the hour.
>
> *Martin Luther*

Success doesn't just enter our lives. It travels best on the right mix of wits and hard work. After opening your mind and taking your first courageous steps towards your goal, the next natural step on the journey up the *Possibility Model* is the production of work. Work is central to the successful implementation of our ideas. It is the necessary link between thought and result. It is the inevitable process through which our volition is transformed into reality.

In most cultures, the correlation between work and success is quite well-internalized. An almost universal understanding on work is that you get nothing if you do nothing. A common belief among modern Christian, Muslim, Jewish and Confucian societies alike is that if you work hard you shall have, at some point, what you desire.

The focus of this basic belief is that a good amount of work is paramount and that God indeed helps those who actively help themselves. However, the relationship of the quantity of work to the production of positive results is not so straightforward.

In many of the Western work environments I have experienced, the modern wisdom about the relationship between work and success is that you should work smarter rather than harder. On the positive side, one can interpret this expression as delivering an important message on the futility of putting in long hours and investing large amounts of energy in a way that does not produce optimal results. It also underlines the importance of intelligence in creating work efficiencies and enhancing productivity.

This phrase has received, however, more negative interpretations. It is sometimes used as a justification for cutting corners or encouraging various levels of procrastination. In highly developed economies with generations of younger workers used to a high standard of living, the temptation to minimize the importance of the time and effort required to achieve goals is growing.

The reality is that you should work smarter *and* harder to be successful in an increasingly competitive global marketplace. In addition to effort and intelligence, the fostering of a positive work culture is also an important driver of success. This chapter will introduce the concept of work utility and present the factors that affect the relationship between work and success. The chapter will also look at each work utility formula variable from a Finnish perspective. It will present the ways and means by which Finnish culture has contributed to enviably high levels of work utility. The end of this chapter shall also present some of the main challenges for the sustainability of high work utility in Finland.

3.1 A working formula

In addition to the raw contribution of effort, there are other important factors that create higher levels of work utility. Work utility is the level at which an input of work contributes to the completion of a given task. It is a product of work effort times the combined effect of work intelligence and the existing work culture. Figure 3-1 presents this simple formula for work utility and its three main variables: effort, intelligence and culture.

FIGURE 3-1: **The work utility formula**

The formula suggested here proposes that work utility is the product of effort times the sum of work intelligence and culture. Effort, intelligence and culture therefore form the main elements of work utility, and these elements are ultimately three important drivers of success. The equation is, of course, much more philosophical than mathematical. It essentially indicates that things like time, personal energy, intelligence and technology are not the only factors leading to higher work utility. Indeed, as most work is conducted with others to produce collective results in any given market, the cultural context and dynamics of where the work is done are also an important part of the equation.

As in neo-classical economics, the model of rational, self-interested human behavior can be considered as only partly correct in explaining or predicting economic success. Adam Smith argued that economic life is deeply embedded in social life, and cannot be understood apart from the customs, morals and habits of the society in which it occurs.[1] This is similar to the claim made here in the context of work utility. The quantitative contribution of work times and the use of intelligent processes and technologies won't always give you the desired outcome in terms of work utility. The cultural environment can be said to play a significant role in ensuring a higher return on the invested effort.

Effort

Effort is indeed the first factor we look at when we examine a work process. Referring to our work utility formula above, if the effort invested is equal to zero, the resulting work utility shall also be equal to zero. In this respect, the formula is in line with the working ideal of many traditional cultures that believe you get nothing if you do nothing.

The amount of time and energy needed to attain a goal varies considerably. This depends on the nature of the objective, the level of initial talent and the resources available. In this respect it is interesting to note some of the work done by Anders Ericsson on the amount of work required to become an expert in any given field.[2] His research is taken up in Malcolm Gladwell's popular book *Outliers*. Gladwell argues that expertise in any area is attained by investing an average of 10 000 hours of effort. He calls this the 10 000 Hour Rule.

Gladwell claims that greatness requires enormous time, using the source of The Beatles' musical talents and Bill Gate's computer proficiency as examples. The Beatles performed live in Hamburg, Germany over 1 200 times from 1960 to 1964, amassing more than 10 000 hours of playing time, therefore meeting the 10 000 Hour Rule. Gladwell asserts that all of the time The Beatles spent performing shaped their talent. Bill Gates met the 10 000 Hour Rule when he gained access to a high school computer in 1968 at the age of 13, and spent 10 000 hours programming on it. Gladwell explains that reaching the 10 000 Hour Rule, which he considers the key to success in any field, is simply a matter of practicing a specific task that can be accomplished with 20 hours of work per week for 10 years.[3]

The learning of a language also offers a clear example of how much raw effort becomes a prerequisite for the attainment of a particular goal. The State Department of the United States, like many other foreign offices, has a set of standard courses for a speaker of English wanting to become functional in another language. The time investment required is indicated upon the assumption that the applicant is starting from scratch in the desired language. For a speaker of English, the full length of courses for mainstream Indo-European languages such as French or German ranges from 5 to 6 months of full-time study. For a language such as

Finnish, which is not an Indo-European language, the time required is closer to one full year. With more challenging languages for the average English speaker, such as Chinese or Arabic, the time investment to be functional in speaking, reading and writing the new language is well over 18 months.

These two examples give us a measure of the range of time needed for most humans to acquire new skills. As we can see, the range of effort required is quite wide: from 1000 hours for becoming at least functional in a foreign language to 10 000 hours for becoming experts in a particular field, as accomplished by Mr. McCartney or Mr. Gates. There are two points to note here. One is that there is indeed no way to escape the minimum requirements of time and effort needed to learn something new and valuable. The other is that to become really proficient and among those whom we may call "professionals" in an occupation, the amount of effort required can represent a significant part of your lifetime.

The reference to genius learners who need little or no investment of effort to reach similar goals is a much romanticized myth of many Hollywood movies. From *Rain Man* to *A Beautiful Mind*, the portrayal of individuals with extraordinary learning powers is there to make audiences dream of the possibility of skills acquired naturally, without the inconvenience of investing time and effort.

In my opinion, this type of fiction may be a de-motivating illusion for the many who are led to believe that regardless of the time invested, they shall never be as proficient as those exceptional beings who need a great deal less learning time. In reality, most people need to invest a significant amount of effort to learn something new. Of course, intellectual abilities and backgrounds vary significantly in the population, but as a rule there is very little substitute for the minimum amount of effort required for performing a given task or even learning the basics of a particular subject.

Intelligence

Intelligence is the second important variable in the work utility formula. It is the great enhancer of individual effort, which in turn produces better work utility. For the same amount of effort invested, intelligence can produce a work utility level that is a factor of what it would be without it. By intelligence here, I mean the use of processes and technologies that have shrunk the amount of individual effort needed to complete certain tasks.

A trip from Helsinki to Paris by plane instead of by car or train cuts the travel time by a factor of 30. Shoveling large amounts of snow with a simple shovel takes roughly 20 times longer than with a Bobcat tractor. In the field of industry, efficient processes and advanced technologies are at the heart of companies' competitive advantages because they can significantly shrink the time and the costs of production. We know that the average car is produced in less than 13 hours in Japan but takes over 22 hours in the United States. This makes it clear that Japanese manufacturers have designed processes and used technologies that produce higher work utility levels. If a Finnish mobile phone manufacturer can produce a high-end mobile phone for less than 50 Euros a unit but its American counterpart has to spend over 80 Euros a unit, the same conclusions in terms of work utility apply. Work intelligence is thus the main driver of productivity and creates efficiencies that are the basis for maintaining competitive advantages.

Culture

Finally, the prevailing work culture is the third important factor in the attainment of higher levels of work utility. The literature on the impact of culture on economic life in general is very rich and diverse. Most of the written word on this subject seems to revolve around the work of one man: Max Weber. He is the author of the seminal *Protestant Ethic and the Spirit of Capitalism*. For Weber, culture was the force behind certain types of economic behavior such as capitalism. This famous German sociologist was the most eminent opponent of another well-known German intellectual, Karl Marx. For Marx, capitalism was the cause of cultural phenomena such as religion. For Weber, religion and the people's "spirit" formed the root of the capitalist economic model.

The term "work ethic," frequently used in post-Weberian literature, comes from his research on the Protestant Ethic. One of his most famous theories is that Protestant cultures have encouraged personality traits that generate a greater inclination for hard work and effort. He goes on to state that in addition to this cultural propensity for work, the spirit of capitalism is founded on other values such as frugality and the desire to master one's environment through innovation and work.

For understandable reasons, Max Weber's work is a staple for much of the modern sociological and philosophical discourse in the Anglo-Saxon, Germanic and Nordic cultural communities. It is less so in the scientific communities of Catholic countries such as France or Italy. This is most likely because his perception of the world put Protestantism on a pedestal. In Finland, Weber's theories hit a particular soft spot because many of the cultural virtues he identifies are also a pervasive part of Finnish culture.[4]

Like many Germans, the Finns share certain Protestant values: the propensity to save, rationality in solving problems, and a focus on daily realities as opposed to celestial abstractions. In terms of generating world-class work utility levels, I argue later in this chapter that modern Finnish society holds two other cultural traits that are particularly conducive to high work utility and success. They are the existence and fostering of high levels of trust and the prioritization of personal well-being in general and of the workplace in particular.

3.2 The Finnish cult of work

Life here is hard work
And it rarely comes with any luck
This is something only a Finn understands

Kari Tapio: Olen Suomalainen
(I am a Finn – Famous Finnish popular song)

Work is a respected and almost celebrated value in Finnish society. Finns attach especially great value to the time and effort invested in the completion of a wide variety of tasks that cause a good brow-sweat. A person's work is her bond to the community and plays a major role in forging the social identity of a Finn. The importance of hard work is deeply rooted in Finnish history and geography. The challenges of a daunting climate, the paucity of easily transformable natural resources and a sparsely inhabited country are all clear historical factors that explain the critical importance of having each member of the community be a highly productive worker. For most of Finland's history, this was a question of survival. You work or you perish.

The Protestant Reformation of the 16th century brought Europeans a new perspective on work. The two key religious leaders of this period were the German theologian Martin Luther and the French theologian Jean Calvin. Finland slowly adopted the teachings of Martin Luther through the Reformation of the Church of Sweden during the 16th century . The doctrinal reformation of the Finnish Church took place during the episcopate of Mikael Agricola, the Bishop of the dioceses of Turku, who had studied at the University of Wittenberg under Martin Luther. He translated the New Testament and large portions of the Old Testament into Finnish.

Luther was an Augustinian friar who grew disenchanted with the Catholic Church and became a leader within the Protestant movement. He believed that people could serve God through their work, that professions were useful, that work was the universal basis of society and the cause of differing social classes, and that people should work diligently in their own occupation and should not try to change from the profession to which they were born. The major point on which Luther differed from the medieval concept of work was in his belief that no type of work was inherently superior to any other.

Luther regarded the monastic and contemplative life, held up as the ideal during the middle ages, as an egotistic and compassionless exercise on the part of the monks, and he accused them of evading their duty to their neighbors. For Luther, a person's vocation was equated to his calling, but all callings were of equal spiritual dignity. This belief was significant because it affirmed the dignity of manual labor.[5]

After the Second World War – or for Finland, after the Continuation War against the Soviet Union and the shorter Lapland War against the Germans – the Finnish appetite for work was put to the full test. The hefty war reparations imposed by the Soviet Union placed an incredible strain on the Finnish work regimen. Totally new infrastructure, including new factories, industrial plants producing textiles, pulp and paper, metal products and ships, needed to be built nearly from scratch. During this period Finland, like post-war Japan, operated on a six-day work week. The

intensive national work regimen continued until 1966. Once again, Finns were working for their survival. This time it was not a battle against a freezing winter on the farm but a fight to maintain their dearly-earned independence through a national outburst of hard work that affected everyone.

For Pekka Lundmark, the CEO of Konecranes, a global Finnish supplier of industrial cranes with a global turnover of over 1.5 billion Euros, this particular phase of the country's history is the most significant Finnish achievement of the past hundred years.[6] The rapid and massive industrialization of Finland, which brought it from a fairly rural and marginal nation to one of the world's most industrialized and technically advanced countries, is indeed extraordinary.

In addition, the egalitarian structure of Finnish society has generated a more uniform value of work, where even the people who are better off economically or more educated take solemn pride in all kinds of manual labor. Many high-level Finnish politicians and business leaders often seek media publicity for the relish they show in running their farms or engaging in physical labor. Manual labor scores points with the electorate in Finland. Many top executives in global companies like Nokia and Wärtsilä enjoy telling their peers how they have built their own house or fixed their own car or boat. The comments exude pride in the mastery of a demanding piece of manual labor, and come from people who have relatively high social positions and higher levels of university education.

One of the icons of Finnish industry, Pekka Herlin, the CEO of the Kone Corporation during the 1970's and 1980's, was always torn between the life of a global corporation leader and the life of a farmer.[7] He was the second generation of Herlins to lead the Kone Corporation, a global manufacturer of elevators, during a critical time of international corporate consolidation.[8] Because of this attachment to the land and perhaps due to the religious background of the country, there is definitely more of a down-to-earth and hands-on work culture throughout Finnish society than in similarly urbanized centers of continental Europe or North America.

Today, the high standard of living enjoyed by the Finns of the baby boomer generation and their children is partly the result of the incredible work ethic of the post-war generation. Though the benefits of wealth have also brought with them the challenge of maintaining a similar work ethic among the younger generation, the Finnish workplace is still by and large an environment where most Finns willingly invest a good part of their existence. Some Finnish workplace gurus, such as Jari Sarasvuo, have recently sounded the national alarm on the paucity of work performed in Finnish companies. Relative to the Finland of yesteryear he may be right, but from a recent comparative European study on the time spent at work, Finns are still close to the top of the charts of the most industrious European nations.[9]

The results of this hard work can be seen in the international success of many Finns in their respective areas of expertise. The investment in education, the availability of resources and a solid work ethic have made legions of Finns international leaders in a host of professional areas. While the list of internationally successful Finns would be too long to reproduce here, this book pays tribute to many of them. Since its independence, Finland has boasted heroes of work utility in a wide variety of fields, from the great Olympian Paavo Nurmi to the software entrepreneur Linus Torvalds.

As further examples of work-related accomplishments, I think that two other high profile areas of human activity, very different from each other, are worth pointing out here. Finnish professionals have been over-represented at the top of the fields of international classical music and motor sports.

Indeed, the cream of the list of the world's leading conductors certainly includes Esa-Pekka Salonen and Jukka-Pekka Saraste. Salonen conducted both the London and Los Angeles philharmonic orchestras during his career. Saraste, who is Salonen's colleague from the famous Sibelius Academy of Helsinki, has led the prestigious philharmonic orchestras of Toronto, Oslo and Cologne. A rising star in conducting is another Finn, Susanna Mälkki, who has made impressive debuts at the St. Louis and Boston Symphonic Orchestras. These conductors are all the students of one of the world's most accomplished teachers of orchestral conducting: Jorma Panula.

In operatic singing, two other Finnish names are among the most respected globally: Karita Mattila, the colorful soprano, and Matti Salminen, the charismatic and powerful bass singer. Following in the line of the great music composers such as Jean Sibelius and Oskar Merikanto are several new talents, including Kaija Saariaho, who won a Grammy Award for Best Opera Recording in 2011.

In an entirely different field, Finns have regularly dominated the field of international motor sports. Keke Rosberg, Mika Häkkinen and Kimi Räikkönen are all Formula One world champions who have become household names for their tens of millions of fans around the world. At the height of his Formula One career Kimi Räikkönen was the best-paid athlete in the world after Tiger Woods. On the rally car circuit, Finnish domination of the sport is even more apparent. Ari Vatanen, Juha Kankkunen, Tommi Mäkinen and Marcus Grönholm have together won eleven World Rally Championships in the past thirty years, making Finland one of the most successful rally car nations in the world.

In both classical music and motor sports, the time and effort required to reach international heights is tremendous. In addition to talent, mastery in these fields comes from endless repetition on a slow and steady journey to the top of your art. Of course, along with its solid work ethic, Finland also offered these great professionals access to the necessary intellectual and practical resources that accelerate your journey to success. In the case of top musicians, it is the access to high-level music education. In the case of motor sports, it is access to good motor engineering and an environment filled with long, often icy and deserted country roads.

3.3 A wealth of wits

Truly great madness cannot be achieved without significant intelligence.

Henrik Tikkanen
A well-known Finnish author and artist

The second element of the work utility formula is intelligence. As we have seen, time and effort are the necessary conditions for high levels of work utility but they do not, on their own, guarantee high work performance. Indeed, work intelligence is the motor of modern competitiveness. Despite the good appetite for work existing in modern Finland, the amount of working time per capita in the country is a little under the OECD average. Working hours per capita are actually significantly less than in Korea, Greece and Hungary, which are all at the top of the OECD Working Hours Index.[10]

The better measure of a country's work utility level can arguably be determined by its ranking on the Global Competitiveness Index. Highly competitive countries can be said to be the leaders in work utility because they produce more and better products per capita than their peers. Their work is especially enhanced by innovation and a positive working culture. In 2010, the top ten countries of the Global Competitiveness Index were the ones listed in Figure 3-2.[11]

The ten most competitive nations in the world are listed in Figure 3-2 along with their ranking in the OECD average working time index. With the notable exception of the United States, most of these countries are far from the top of the most industrious nations' index. One can even conclude that the nations like Switzerland, Germany and the Netherlands, because of their high competitiveness

FIGURE 3-2:

Top ten competiveness and working hours rankings

Country	Competitiveness Ranking	Working Hours Ranking
Switzerland	1	33
Sweden	2	20
Singapore	3	–
United States	4	8
Germany	5	27
Japan	6	12
Finland	7	16
Netherlands	8	28
Denmark	9	22
Canada	10	13

ranking despite their relatively low working hours ranking, are particularly "intelligent" and boast strong technology-driven and innovative work processes. This means that they are the world leaders in getting more economic results out of less work. Finland, with its enviable 7th position in the Global Competitiveness Index, is more akin to Japan and even the United States, where high work utility seems to depend on a balanced mix of hard work and intelligence.

The rankings of the hardest-working nations on earth in relation to their competitiveness are more telling. As can be seen from Figure 3-3, almost all of the world's top 10 hardest-working nations are relative laggards in terms of competitiveness and work utility. The most extreme

FIGURE 3-3:

Top ten working hours and competitiveness rankings

Country	Working Hours Ranking	Competitiveness Ranking
Korea	1	22
Greece	2	83
Hungary	3	52
Poland	4	39
Czech Republic	5	36
Mexico	6	66
Italy	7	48
United States	8	4
New Zeeland	9	23
Portugal	10	46

example of this is Greece with a number 2 ranking in working hours but a sobering number 83 ranking in the competitiveness index. This would be a good reference for those Finns and Europeans who believe that they have bailed out Greece from its financial troubles because of the country's poor work ethic. In fact, these numbers indicate that Greeks are working among the hardest but unfortunately far from the smartest in the world. The improvement for them lies in the prospect of enhancing the intelligence, innovation and possibly the culture surrounding their labor. This table reinforces our message on work utility. Working harder does not get you far enough if you don't work smarter.

Finland has done very well in international competitiveness rankings over the past 10 years. It was ranked number one in the World Economic Forum's Global Competitiveness report on two occasions, in 2001 and again in 2005. In 2011, Finland came in fourth. Its position has remained high in the rankings throughout the last decade. The reasons for this have a lot to do with work intelligence. As we have seen in previous chapters, Finland has made important investments in education and in research and development. With close to four percent of the Finnish GNP going into research and development, Finland is among the countries that invest the most per capita in work-enhancing technologies and processes.

Great innovations

Indeed, Finns have been very inventive over the past hundred years. In the first part of the last century two notable Finnish inventors gave a glimpse of what Finnish ingenuity could bring to the world. Artturi Virtanen and Tuomas Vohlonen made their mark through their innovations in the field of agricultural chemistry and modern compasses. Virtanen is the 1945 Nobel Prize winner for his invention of the AIV liquid that is added to green fodder to improve storage. Volhonen's inventions became the basis for the successful company Suunto and their range of high-end sport watches, compasses and heart-rate monitors.

More recently, and more surprisingly, Finns have made inventive strides in health-enhancing innovations in food. The discovery of Xylitol, the natural sweetener that comes from birch, led to the creation of Xylitol-based gum and candies, and has significantly lowered the incidence of dental cavities among its users. With this invention, Finns have altered the widely held belief in the rest of the world that chewing gum and eating candies is bad for your teeth. Finland is also credited for the invention of cholesterol-reducing margarines. Again, a type of food known to be potentially harmful for the heart is actually made helpful and healthy.

In the field of medicine, Finnish innovation has been bountiful. The publicly listed Orion Oyj has been in the pharmaceutical business since 1917. It is the leading company in its field in Finland, with a market share of over 30 percent. It has been particularly successful with the commercialization of drugs that treat heart disease and some forms of cancer. In the field of medical research Finland has been a centre for cutting-edge research for many decades. Ragnar Granit, an eminent Finnish physiologist, won the Nobel Prize in Medicine for his seminal discoveries on the workings of the eye's retina.

Since then, Finnish researchers and practitioners have developed our understanding and come up with solutions for some of the world's most pressing health issues. At the University of Kuopio, Professor Hilkka Soininen has significantly advanced Alzheimer's research. In Tampere, Bioretec has developed a highly innovative bioabsorbable antibiotic screw used to fix broken bones during surgery. This new technique reduces healthcare costs by preventing orthopedic surgery complications. In Turku, the guru of international sport surgeons, Sakari Orava has successfully operated on the limbs of a long list of world-class athletes, including David Beckham and Haile Gebrselassie.

More recently, a promising breakthrough in the search for a cure for cancer has come from the Universities of Tampere and Turku. Under the leadership of academic researcher Jukka Westermarck these researchers have identified a previously unknown mechanism which could be responsible for the onset of cancer. The research team has isolated a protein that causes healthy cells to become cancerous. This discovery may lead to a breakthrough for the treatment of cancer.

Finally, Finnish medicine has also recently tackled one of Finland's most wicked health problems. Biotie, a Finnish drug development company, is planning to launch Nalmefene, a new drug that claims to be a cure for alcoholism. The drug supposedly inhibits brain stimulus that reinforces the desire and craving for alcohol and other addictive substances. We will be discussing later in this book the delicate issue of alcohol usage in Finland. However, it suffices to say here that if this drug can really address alcohol addiction in Finland and elsewhere as it claims, it would definitely qualify as a Finnish Miracle.

Making smart and sustainable products

Finnish products enjoy a solid international reputation. They ranked an enviable 4th position in the Country Brand Index survey in 2009. This is a significant achievement because the top three were the world's three economic Goliaths: Japan, the USA and Germany. Finnish products, coming mostly from the paper, metal and technology industries, are regarded as being of high quality and Finnish companies are perceived to be reliable. It is interesting to note that Finland clearly ranked higher in this index than its other Nordic peers. Where Sweden is especially well-known for its inexpensive, appealing consumer products, Norway for its oil and Denmark for its agriculture, Finland's reputation is based on paper machines, ice-breakers, mobile phones, elevators and forest machinery.

The main strength of Finnish products and services is their sustainability. As with the country's industrial and social policy, Finns believe in product sustainability. In a nutshell, they believe that products should be of good quality and made to last. Products and services are perceived as investments that should provide a decent return over their life-cycle. Reparability and servicing are perceived as huge pluses and most Finns have a natural disdain for the current global throw-awayism in consumer products.

Companies like Marimekko, Iittala and Fiskars pride themselves on the high quality and superior design of their products. They even offer repair services and advice to further enhance durability and customer satisfaction. At the industrial level, the service offerings of the large-scale machinery companies like Kone, Wärtsilä and Konecranes are at the heart of their competitive advantage and profitability. This is because they add years to the use of expensive investments and truly leverage the investments made by their customers.

In this respect, the most successful Finnish companies work harder and smarter. They know that in the long term, customers will want to pay a premium for quality products that last longer. This in turn allows these companies to make investments in the constant development of technical and design innovations that continue to extend the usability of their products at an increasingly reasonable price.

Sporting innovations

The realm of sports gives a rich and concrete set of examples of how greater work utility can be achieved through the use of better intelligence. Indeed, the vast field of sports sciences has made huge advances over the past thirty years in understanding the physical limits and possibilities of the human body in motion. The expanding fields of biomechanics, exercise physiology and sports psychology are filled with thousands of researchers who have dedicated their lives to unlocking the mysteries of the human body in movement.

Perhaps some of the best work in this field had been done by the American College of Sports Medicine (ACSM) and the European College of Sport Science (ECSS). It is interesting to note that one Finn has been a global and respected leader in the field: Professor Paavo V. Komi.

After some forty years of hard work and the use of his considerable intelligence, Prof. Komi became one of the world's top names in biomechanics. He became the President of the International Council of Sport Science (ICSSPE) and then the President of the ECSS. I had the pleasure of serving both as the Secretary General of ICSSPE and as the first Executive Director of the ECSS during his terms of office.

Even in the circles of these advanced scientific disciplines, it is commonly believed that athletes already know what scientists will later confirm to be true. Indeed, many intelligent innovations in sports have been driven by athletes' experimentation and out-of-the-box thinking. In many ways this use of hands-on intelligence is close to the use of intuitive trial and error covered in the previous chapter.

The most famous example of lateral thinking by an elite athlete is the story of Dick Fosbury. Before the 1960's, high jumpers generally leaped over the bar feet-first. A new head-first technique surfaced in the 1960's, with Dick Fosbury as its notable early proponent. Employing his "Fosbury Flop" style, the American earned the gold medal at the 1968 Olympics. Fosbury developed this technique out of necessity. In high school he had difficulties assimilating the then-predominant straddle method. He went back to trying the older upward scissors method. He then experimented with trying to cross the bar going into it headfirst. The results were encouraging and he perfected his technique with a J-shaped approach that gave more speed and power to his liftoff.

When he first made it to the NCAA national championships, some in the media ridiculed him and his "back flop" by coining him the laziest jumper in the world. He ultimately proved the skeptics wrong by winning the gold medal in Mexico with an Olympic and American record of 2.24 meters. Though he had made significant improvements on the results of most previous Olympic jumpers of the last century, he also laid the foundation for a quantum leap of improvement in modern high jumping, with almost all high jumpers adopting his technique after the Mexico Games. After some stagnation of the world record in the 50's and 60's, the bar for elite high jump rose to the current world record of 2.45 meters, set by Javier Sotomayor in 1993.

Another well-known sporting innovation is the V-style ski jumping technique. Ski jumping comes from Norway and became a big sport in most of the Nordic countries and in many central European countries during the 20th century. Japan came in later, mostly during the 1990's, with some excellent ski jumpers. Like the Fosbury flop, the new V-style technique was also developed by an athlete, Jan Boklöv from Sweden, in 1985. Until then, ski jumpers would jump off their frighteningly high take-off ramps with their skis parallel to each other. This was called the Daescher technique. By putting his skis in a V shape facing outwards, Boklöv noticed that he could fly significantly farther.

Despite this, elite ski jumpers did not widely adopt this technique until the early 1990's. Even the most successful Finnish Olympic athlete after Paavo Nurmi, and the most successful ski jumper of all time, Matti Nykänen,[12] won 3 gold medals at the winter Olympic Games in Calgary in 1988 using the traditional Daescher technique. One of the first athletes to successfully internalize the new V-style technique was another Finnish ski jumper, Toni Nieminen. He won the gold medal at the Winter Olympic Games of Alberville in

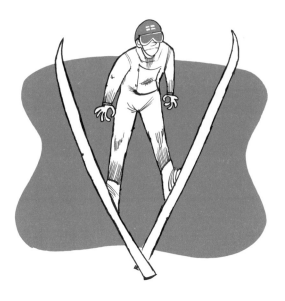

1992 and became the youngest gold medalist in the history of the Winter Olympic Games at the tender age of 16. His mastery of the V-style allowed him, in 1994, to make the first over-200-meters jump in the history of the sport. The V-style has now become the norm in this discipline and has improved general results and length of jumps by approximately 10 percent.

In the world of motorbike racing, one Finnish name has remained a legend for over 40 years. Jarno Saarinen is the most successful Finnish motorbike racer of all time. He developed the famous "hang-off" technique, which allows motorbike racers to take sharper and faster curves by hanging off or dragging their knee to the point that they almost touch the ground. This increases the natural limits of the motorcycle and its tires. From the early 1900's to around 1970 every rider raced with knees tucked in firmly on either side of the gas tank. It was Jarno Saarinen who revolutionized the world of Motorcyle Grand Prix with his new technique in the early 1970's. All of the world's best racers quickly adopted the technique, including Kenny Roberts and Paul Smart. The technique has become standard in the sport since then.

To come up with this innovation, Saarinen combined two competitive strengths that are very Finnish. His first Finnish strength was that he was very well educated in technical matters. He was a mechanical engineer and thus could modify his bike to his needs. The second was his winter expertise. He began his career as an ice racer and developed a sense for taking slanted curves with his bike. The result of these personal features is an innovation that changed an entire sport with a new speed-enhancing technique.

Saarinen had a brilliant yet dramatically short career. At the age of 25, just graduated as an engineer, he entered the highly competitive world of Grand Prix motorbike racing. Between 1971 and 1973, Saarinen won a total of 15 Grand Prix events, along with the 250cc World Championships in 1972. In the same year he finished second in the 350cc World Championships, giving defending champion Giacomo Agostini a formidable challenge. In 1973 he became the first European rider to win the prestigious Daytona 200 race in the United States using a lower-capacity motorbike. The same year, he jumped to an early lead in the 500cc Grand Prix Championships, then the premier racing class.

His 1973 season ended in tragedy in Monza, Italy. A failure to clean up an oil stain on the fastest track in the circuit caused his talented rival Renzo Pasolini to fall in front of Saarinen. Saarinen was unable to avoid Pasolini, and the resulting crash caused a multiple rider pileup. In all, 14 riders were involved in the mayhem that resulted. When the dust cleared, Saarinen and Pasolini lay dead, with many others seriously injured. Races were banned at Monza

soon after that. Jarno Saarinen's legacy continued to live on, especially in Italy, where his first name Jarno became a popular name for newborn boys during the 1970's. One of these boys is Jarno Trulli, the well-known driver on the current Formula 1 circuit.

More recently, Finns have received a massive boost in national pride, partly assisted by a sporting innovation. Until 2011, Finland had won only one World Championship in ice hockey. It was a sweet victory in 1995 against the country's arch-rival and neighbor, Sweden. Even more strikingly, this victory happened in the heart of Swedish ice hockey, at the Stockholm Globe Arena. The entire country lost its senses and the market square in Helsinki swelled with over 100 000 people celebrating in delirious nationalistic joy. Though my native Canada has won these championships 18 times in the history of the sport, I had never seen such a display of collective national pride and joy triggered by a mere ice hockey victory.

This level of exuberance occurred again when the Finnish team won the World Championships in 2011. As fate would have it, Finns would once more defeat their "favorite" team Sweden, and would crush the Swedes with a devastating score of 6–1. I believe that the Finns, having come to these finals a total of eight times and having taken the top prize only once, simply decided to play smarter and harder. This time, the team spirit and the relaxed yet focused attitude of the players rose to a higher level than in the past. In addition, the Finnish team got a boost from one remarkable sporting innovation: the Air Crank. In the critical semi-final match against Russia, the young Mikael Granlund scored an unbelievable first goal that left the Russian goalie completely helpless. He took the puck on top of his stick while coming at full speed behind the net and just slung the puck in mid-air right into the high corner of the net. This had never been done in such a spectacular way in the entire history of the World Championships. The young Granlund had put a lot of effort and intelligence into mastering this new technique, and it paid off in a big way.

3.4 A culture of trust and well-being

As we have seen, Finland holds many cultural virtues that contribute to a high level of work utility. From a Weberian perspective, the Protestant values of thrift, pragmatism and ingenuity are certainly a boost to the Finnish national work-utility level. I believe the Finland of today also benefits from two other widespread national values that give it a particular competitive advantage. These are the existence and mainte-nance of very high levels of social trust and the prioritization of personal well-being.

Honest as a Finn

Social trust is the glue that makes modern societies work. In societies where there are low levels of trust, business processes tend to be slow and costly. In countries where social trust is high, deals are made quickly, execution is flexible and litigation is rare. In countries where there are low levels of social trust, commercial deals are complicated, contracts are painfully long, execution is rigid and litigation is rife. High social trust societies are faster and use the work of their people in more efficient ways than their low trust society counterparts.

An interesting international Gallup Poll on social trust asked the people of several different countries how many would trust a complete stranger. In a survey conducted by British sociologist David Halpern he found that only 34 percent of Americans believe that other people can be trusted. In Latin America, the number is only 23 percent and in Africa the figure falls to 18 percent. This figure in all the Nordic countries, including Finland, is close to 70 percent.[13] In Britain the figure is a surprising 29 percent, down from 60 percent four decades ago. These figures represent a simple yet important indicator of the pool of trust existing in a given society.

In 2007, another Gallup Poll asked people from 86 countries to express their level of trust in other citizens. To help gauge levels of trust in a context-specific situation, Gallup asked respondents whether it was likely that a neighbor, the police or a stranger would return their lost wallet or valuables to them. On both questions related to the neighbor and the police, Finnish respondents ranked number one in the world, with positive trust percentages of 94 percent for their neighbors and 98 percent for the Finnish police. On

the chances of a stranger returning the wallet, Finns were slightly more skeptical, but still ranked a respectable 5th in the world, with a positive response rate of 31 percent.[14]

My first discovery of Finland's important trust reserve came from a course I taught in Anglo-American law at the Helsinki Court of Appeals in the early 1990's. I found that my students, the judges of the Court of Appeals, were generally much more relaxed and flexible in their reasoning than their American and even Canadian counterparts. One reason for this is clearly the lower level of litigation per capita in Finland versus the increasingly litigious North American societies.

In the United States, there are 391 litigation lawyers for every 100 000 citizen. In Finland there are more than ten times fewer litigation lawyers, with 36 litigation lawyers per capita.[15] The number of litigation lawyers is also high in places like the United Kingdom and Australia and low in places like Japan and Canada. The amount of litigation lawyers per capita correlates to a certain extent with the level of litigation and relative size of the awards. This in turn has an impact on the cost of insurance and ultimately on the cost and general fluidity of contractual business processes. Lower-level litigation societies like Finland, Japan and Canada thus have a trust-related competitive advantage over more litigation prone societies like the United States or the United Kingdom. The rise of litigation in the United States imposes a heavy and futile tax on the workings of the market and a significant drain on national work utility formulas. A litigious working culture clearly reduces the level of work efficiency and work utility.

Another measure of the high trust social environment existing in Finland is the perception of public sector integrity. According to the Corruption Perceptions Index (CPI) published by Transparency International, Finland is one of the least corrupt nations in the world.[16] This study is conducted in 178 countries every year. It measures the perceived level of public sector corruption. In 2007, Finland was ranked number one in the world. In 2010, Finland was ranked a decent 4th, only one decimal point behind other high trust countries such as Denmark and New Zealand.

One respected writer on the significance of social trust as a catalyst for social and economic development is Francis Fukuyama. He is the acclaimed author of *The End of History* and *The Last Man*. In his book entitled *Trust: The Social Virtues and the Creation of Prosperity*, he claims that high levels of social trust are the reasons why countries like Germany, Japan and even the United States have been so successful economically.

He explains that those societies that have been able to create more trust for others outside of the family (i.e., strangers) and have a dynamic civil society, while successfully fending off the powers of an overly interventionist and controlling state, have been economically successful. He states that only these types of countries can create genuinely global organizations able to work on a large dose of social trust. He states that the Confucian values of China with their strict focus on the importance of families and the state "dirigisme" of countries like France make them less apt in creating global organizations and in generating wealth.[17]

The work of Francis Fukuyama on social trust is of particular interest in the Finnish context. Many of Fukuyama's indicators of a high trust society apply to Finland. First, Finland is by and large a meritocracy. As indicated in the first chapter, the country has a ruthlessly egalitarian structure and has given almost all of its citizens access to high quality education. The result is a corporate culture that values competence over social or family status. Even in the largest family-owned companies, the operational management team is often made up of independent professionals.

A case in point is the Kone Corporation, a world leader in the elevator business that is controlled by the Finnish Herlin family. Though Antti Herlin exercises family control as chairman of the board, the operational and strategic direction of the company was given to Matti Alahuhta, a world-class professional business leader. This out-of-the-family trust is, according to Fukuyama, one of the success factors in building strong and efficient multinational corporations. Finland's Nokia recently took this even one step further by choosing a non-Finn, a Canadian executive, Stephen Elop, to run Nokia, the country's largest multinational corporation.

One area where Finland can be said to have differed from its other high-trust and high growth country peers, such as Germany and Japan, is the relatively high level of state intervention in the national economy. This is indeed true for the post-war period, where national industrial policy was made from the top down and specifically three industrial areas were earmarked for massive state investments: forestry, metal and electronics. This is akin to the economic "dirigisme" of

France that Fukuyama considers harmful for the dynamic development of national economies.

For Finland, the negative effects of a state-controlled policy were mitigated by a few factors. One was the good sense applied by government officials in making industrial policy at that time. These were natural and intelligent choices for the country's development. Another related aspect is the trust of Finns in their institutions. Despite the strong influence of the state in economic affairs, nepotism and self-serving decisions were mostly avoided. Finally, the strength of Finnish civil society has been a strong generator of national institutions and arguably of national trust.

If the theory on social trust from civil society thinkers such as Locke, Tocqueville and Fukuyama hold true, Finland certainly has benefited from a good dose of civil society trust over the past sixty years. The main hypothesis of this theory is that when you have a vibrant civil society you generate more social trust. Civil organizations are made up of people from all walks of life, who are not related to each other and who are working mostly on a voluntary basis for the benefit of a common goal.

The Finnish civil society is strong. The Finnish national register of associations holds 120 000 organizations. These are related to a wide range of human activity, from politics and health to sports and culture. The associations have a combined membership of approximately 15 million persons, which is three times the national population. Approximately 75 percent of Finns are members of some association during their lifetime. In terms of number of civic organizations and voluntary work, Finland is a global leader, along with other Nordic countries and the Netherlands.[18]

In silence we trust

A man is valued by his results, not his words.

Finnish proverb

On the personal level, one of the surprising catalysts of social trust in Finland is the culture of silence. To the casual foreign observer, the Finnish reserve is perhaps the most striking cultural feature of *Finnishness*. Silence is a double-edged sword when it comes to building trust. If used appropriately with a view to actively listening to others, it can be an important creator of trust and thus a catalyst for success. If silence exists because of a refusal or failure to interact with others, then it corrodes trusts and increases the likelihood of failure.

Finns regard those who speak too much with some disdain and even suspicion. They prefer an efficient communication style that is direct and to the point. They often prefer to listen and then speak when someone actually has something interesting or useful to say. They dislike small talk precisely because they do not fully understand or appreciate its function. A person who spends too much time talking is suspected of spending too little time working.

The Finnish affinity for silence can be traced back to the rural roots of most Finns, who often worked on their own or within small groups. Harsh winters and a sparsely inhabited countryside were also factors keeping individuals more isolated than in warm countries like Italy or densely populated countries like Holland. Finns are by nature very private people, who have a more utilitarian relationship to speech than individuals from most other Western countries. Richard D. Lewis describes this relative cultural feature quite well when he states that Finns are "people with a Western set of values cloaked in an Asian communication style."[19]

Surprisingly, the silence culture of Finland often provides a set of positive opportunities for establishing trust and creating success. Silence creates the social space for the all-important art of listening. Many Asian cultures point out than humans have two ears and only one mouth for a reason. Finns have strongly internalized this belief. They are generally masters of the art of listening before speaking. They often take their time to understand and diagnose what a person has to say before adding their own voice and creating a dialogue. If you add in the high-level education and the Finnish egalitarian ethic, you obtain a recipe for an extremely economical and well-balanced communication culture.

When everyone gets a chance to be heard, it ensures that a wider base of information is available, which in turn generates more enlightened decisions. This disposition for listening is interestingly embedded in the Finnish language. The word for a speech or verbal address is "puheenvuoro" which literally means "speech turn." The notion that communication in Finland should be taken in turns is a reinforcement of the idea that you should respect a person's moment of speech. In Finland, it is extremely rude to interrupt when someone else is speaking. Finns also frown upon those who take "too many turns" at speaking. This is deemed rude and inefficient.

In business life, the art of listening is critical. In an article published and reprinted in the *Harvard Business Review*, management guru Peter Drucker lists eight practices of effective executives. At the end, he concludes: "We just reviewed eight practices of effective executives. I'm going to throw in one final bonus practice. This one is so important that I will elevate it to a rule: Listen first, speak last."[20] Jorma Ollila, the Chairman of the Nokia Corporation, has often commented that the corporate culture of the company has always been one where anyone at any level of the organization can voice an opinion.

Listening is the foundation for creating trust and winning more business. In his book *The Speed of Trust*, Stephen M.R. Covey identifies the behavior of listening first as a critical factor in successful organizations: "Smart organizations recognize the power of Listen first, particularly as it pertains to customers and other external stakeholders. If companies don't do market research to determine the needs and preferences of consumers *before* they produce products, they don't make money."[21]

The challenge with Finland's culture of silence is that it is frequently taken too far. The propensity to work alone, communicative risk aversion and the fear of saying something not "useful enough," sometimes lead to unfortunate breakdowns in communication. We shall come back to this a little later in the chapter.

Gambling on trust

The combined success of the Finnish public lotteries is another good example of the essential part social trust can play in producing superior economic results. The two largest state-controlled lotteries, Veikkaus and RAY, produce roughly one billion Euros a year for admirable national causes. That is equivalent to over 200 Euros per citizen. This is five times higher than the European average.[22] The net income coming from the operation of public lotteries represents around 5 percent of the national personal income tax pool. Though some countries may have higher levels of gambling per capita, the transparency and efficiency in ensuring a generous bottom line for charitable causes is unmatched in Europe.

By contrast, if we take the example of Russia and its top three lottery operators, we notice an entirely different story.

In this country of 140 million people, the annual turnover of the top lottery operators together is just over 100 million Euros per annum. This would seem to equate to much less than one Euro per capita in lottery earnings in Russia, versus close to 200 Euros per capita in lottery earnings in Finland. Leaving general social and economic differences aside, I think that one of the main explanatory factors for this huge gap is a lack of general trust.

In the times of the Soviet Union, lotteries were organized by the state. These turned out to be Orwellian-style fixed draws designed to instill a false sense of hope in the population. This period of Russian history is still fresh in the minds of many Russians and has made most citizens wary of games of chance organized by the state. If you factor in the general distrust that exists among Russians in relation to their public institutions, it is not surprising that the current Russian lotteries find it difficult to attract any customers at all.

In North America, we see that most lottery corporations still do not match the per capita returns of leading European countries like Finland. The public sentiment toward gambling in the United States is generally more negative than it is in Europe. When it comes to playing with money in the United States, an automatic association is made with Las Vegas, loose moral integrity and the industry's historic links to organized crime. This does not contribute to boosting trust levels within the general population. The trust deficit translates into financial under-performance in many American states and even some Canadian provinces.

In Finland, as in several other European countries, the history of organized games of chance is much less tainted with distrust. Most successful lottery or gambling operators have a long and respected history. Many of them are the result of the initiative of the civil society, private non-profit organizations like sports clubs or associations to assist the disabled. Strict governmental control has kept criminality at bay. This is especially true in Finland. Finland's success in this field comes from a compound trust effect. Consumers widely trust that draws are legitimate and citizens at large trust that most of the earnings coming from regulated operators go to legitimate public causes.

Investing in well-being

In North America and especially in the United States the word "welfare" seems to have become an extremely negative term in political and social discourse. Indeed, Americans seem to be ferociously divided on the question of who should pay the increasing costs of education, health services and housing.

In Finland, as we have seen, the state provides free world-class education for all its citizens. It also gives free access to good healthcare and makes sure that all citizens have a roof over their head. On top of all this, standard vacations are five weeks per year, and that doesn't include bank holidays. The natural question that pops up for most foreign observers mind is: How can they afford it? How can a country with such a fiscal burden remain on top of the Global Competitiveness Index year after year? The answer is that, in truth, Finland cannot afford not to make these significant investments in its citizens' well-being.

Finland was not always a world leader in collective well-being. Indeed, in the late 19th century the country suffered from relative poverty. The most notable low point came in the famine years of 1866 to 1868. A natural famine struck and wiped out over 15 percent of the population. The Grand Duchy of Finland was ill-equipped financially and logistically to react to the disaster.

The level of wealth per capita in Finland remained low for the entire first half of the 20th century. It is only after the Second World War that the GNP per capita started to grow impressively, by a factor of six times over a period of fifty years. We have seen that this was due to the rapid industrialization of the country. Indeed, in the 1960's Finland experienced one of the fastest rates of rural depopulation among Western industrialized nations. Over a period of 10 years, 600 000 people were added to the urban population, and the urbanization rate (the proportion of people living in urban areas) increased from 38.4 percent in 1960 to 50.9 percent in 1970.

What is important to note here is that the massive investments made in infrastructure were matched by massive new investments in the personal well-being of Finnish citizens. Only then did real educational, health and personal logistics support begin to be widely available to the Finnish population. This was seen not merely as a cost but also as a necessary investment in the productivity potential of the nation. The massive outlays of capital by the state were not made on the basis of a philosophical or religious belief of equality or even charity. Rather, they were a clear strategic move to develop the country into a sustainable western economic force. Finns understood then that their future fortunes were embedded in the country's human capital.

More recently, some studies have sought to better understand the link between human well-being and competitiveness. In a study commissioned by the City of Espoo[23], Professor Antti Hautamäki reports on the natural synergy existing among human well-being, productivity, innovation and competitiveness. He defends and proposes new avenues for the development the Capital Area's well-being infrastructure as a necessity for the maintenance of the region's competitive advantage. It is all quite intuitive. Happy, healthy and well-educated citizens are in a better position to produce the innovations needed for the sustainable competitiveness of the nation.

The Finnish model of promoting well-being as an enhancer of sustainable innovation is also taken up by a celebrated young professor named Pekka Himanen. He was the youngest-ever PhD in Finland, at the tender age of 20. His books on the information society have been translated into several languages worldwide. In his book *The Information Society and the Welfare State: The Finnish Model*,[24] Himanen provides great academic insight into the workings and performance of Finland as a world-class innovation center. He claims that Finland and its fully fledged welfare state are not incompatible with technological innovation and with a dynamic and competitive economy. On the contrary, investment in well-being is a decisive contributing factor for the growth of the Finnish economy on a stable basis. It supplies the human foundation for productivity, through the use of considerable tax income to maintain social services and general quality of life.

Himanen notes that Finland stands in sharp contrast to the Silicon Valley model, which is entirely driven by market mechanisms, individual entrepreneurial activity and the culture of risk. Compared to the Finnish model, the Silicon Valley approach comes with considerable social costs, including acute social inequality and a deteriorating basis for both locally generated human capital and economic infrastructure.

This development of the culture of well-being has thus been an essential part of working smarter towards greater levels of national work-utility and sustainable competitiveness. This is how many leading nations like Finland and other Nordic countries, all of which make significant investments in social well-being, remain competitive. They turn the cost of community well-being into an investment for lasting economic strength.

3.5 Working the Nokia way

Perhaps the most impressive and certainly the best-known success story of Finland is that of the Nokia Corporation.[25] We have alluded to elements of Nokia's success earlier and we shall continue to do so later in our journey up the Possibility Model. Nokia's success, like all success stories, can be looked at from many angles. From the viewpoint of the Possibility Model, there would be something valuable to learn from the Nokia experience at each of the five levels. The Nokia story is emphasized here because I believe that at the heart of many of the company's successes is a long history of exceptionally high levels of work utility.

Mr. Anssi Vanjoki, a former Vice-President of Nokia and one of the company's leading figures of the past 20 years, explains the company's past success in simple terms.[26] He states that the roots of Nokia's achievements can be traced to the company's creation in 1865 by a 25-year-old engineer, Fredrik Idestam. Vanjoki's view is that from the outset, the Nokia Corporation had a special way of working that was and remained part of its operational DNA. It has had a constant ability to reinvent itself and find fresh ways of commercializing new technologies.

Nokia's early days

Vanjoki's insight certainly holds true in the case of Idestam. This young Finn was a graduate student in metal engineering in the Harz Mountains in Germany. By pure coincidence and without the authorization of the manufacturing plant's director, he was able to observe a new process for producing paper. The innovation belonged to Heinrich Voelter and consisted of adding 20–25 percent more wood pulp to the processing mix instead of linen, which had been used up till then. The process produced paper faster and cheaper.

With linen prices high and demand for paper rising rapidly in those days, the nascent Nokia was already placing itself in a winning position. Idestam understood that in his native forest-rich Finland, the process would constitute a real money-making machine. He obtained a license from the Finnish Senate and immediately ordered Voelter machines for two new plants: one for the city of Tampere, and one for the city of Nokia, the place from which the company ultimately derived its name.

It is interesting to note that even at this stage, Nokia was using and developing world-class technology. Idestam developed the company's manufacturing process further by using a new kind of paper pulp that made it possible to increase its share of the resulting paper products. Idestam presented the new paper pulp invention at the Paris World's Fair in 1867 and was awarded the bronze medal for his invention. Interestingly, Voelter's general paper mill process was awarded the gold medal at the same event. This is how the culture of using and continuously improving cutting-edge technology from Finland and abroad became a part of the Nokia DNA.

The Finnish civil war of 1918 left scars on many Finns. Because of these trying times, the CEO of the Nokia Corporation at that time, Gustaf Fogelholm, wished to move into early retirement and sell his shares in his paper mill business. Eduard Polón, the main owner of the neighboring Finnish Rubber Factory, along with a few of his partners, decided to seize the opportunity and buy Fogelholm's shares. This made them the controlling owners of the Nokia Corporation's paper mill business by the end of 1918.

The rubber works company made galoshes, boots and shoes for the international market. The beginning of World

War I brought about a sudden disruption in the rubber products landscape. Many competitors disappeared. High inflation also helped the rubber company become profitable. This good fortune allowed Polón and his associates to continue their expansion by buying a cable factory in 1922, one that had been established by Arvid Wikström a decade earlier.

Wikström was another young engineer, only 26-years-old, and had studied in England and Germany. It was in Germany that he, like Idestam before him, decided to bring back to Finland what he had learned about industrial cable production. His company did well at the outset. He was a very hands-on CEO, often showing up in overalls and mixing with his group of workers at the plant. The company ran into difficulties when the First World War made it difficult to access raw materials from the international market. These challenges were Eduard Polón's opportunity and made the acquisition of the cable factory business possible.

It is interesting to note that Eduard Polón was once ordered to be deported to Siberia for sending one of his sons to military training in Germany against the interests of the Russian Empire. He had to flee his Helsinki home and lead his business from remote villages in Russia. Finally, these three companies, producing paper, rubber products and industrial cables, furnished the three main manufacturing legs of the Nokia industrial conglomerate from the early 1920's to almost the early 1990's. The brains behind the financial engineering of these acquisitions, Eduard Polón, became one of the wealthiest and most respected businessmen in Helsinki until the end of his life.

The roots of the modern Nokia Corporation as a telecom technology provider can be traced to its cable and energy businesses. Indeed, in the 1930's, the company received substantial state contracts to build the wire infrastructure of the national telephone network. This made the company the supreme cable manufacturer in Finland. After the war, almost six percent of the war debt to the Soviet Union was paid with cables. Thereafter, nearly 25 percent of the company's exports went to the Soviet Union.

The company's dependence on raw cable exports to the East caused the CEO of the time, Björn Westerlund, an electrical engineer, to make bold investments in diversifying the business. He wanted to open up the company's possibilities to export new types of developed goods to Western countries. He identified electronics as a sector of the future. In 1958, he established the company's first electronics division. For its first years of operation, this small division mostly imported supercomputers from Germany and England for national resale. This allowed its employees to familiarize themselves with the technology and offer simple computing services to other businesses.

On the way to great success

By the end of the 1960's Nokia was producing its own electronic devices. The most significant and far-reaching initiative was the decision to become competitive in building telephone exchanges. A few decades later, this turned out to be a great source of competitive advantage and synergy with the mobile phone business. From scratch, the company set itself to be a competitor of the then-dominant companies in this area: Ericsson and Siemens.

The company's first portable radio phone device was produced because of a call for tenders from the Finnish army in the early 1960's. Until the end of the 1980's, the electronics division of Nokia was only a very small yet rapidly growing part of Nokia's diversified general business. The creation of open mobile networks from the ARP network of the 1970's to the Nordic NMT network of the 1980's, and finally the international GSM standard, made it possible for Nokia's network and phone products and services to expand exponentially.

During the same period the company was making less fortunate investments in the area of electronics. The most notable of these was a foray into the television business. Nokia bought the Finnish business Salora-Luxor, a manufacturer of television sets. According to Anssi Vanjoki, the entire Finnish television manufacturing enterprise of the 1970's and 80's is one of the Finns' great business failures. The reason was the lack of truly innovative, home-grown technology as well as a lack of economies of scale in production compared to the ultimately victorious producers of Asia.

Though Nokia was still working as a conglomerate of almost 180 different businesses during the 1980's, it was the failure of its television business that almost brought the company to its financial knees, and paradoxically was later the reason for the intelligent and courageous leap of faith to sell off the rubber, cable, pulp and paper as well as all the other electronics divisions of the company in order to focus on telecom networks and devices.

In 1988, the company suffered one of its worst financial losses. Tragically, Nokia's charismatic and innovative CEO, Kari Kairamo, took his own life that year. In 1991, the financial difficulties of the company continued, and the main Nokia shareholders, the two largest banks in Finland, began to consider negotiating the sale of their shares to the company's archrival Ericsson.[27] The parties could not come to an understanding on the specific corporate assets to be sold. Nokia's shareholders wanted the company's worst performing divisions, including the television division, to be a part of the deal. Ericsson refused. Looking back, it is hard to imagine what might have been the impact of that potential sale on the Finnish economy and on the world of telecoms.

In this particular case, one can say that the company's misfortunes ultimately became the source of its salvation. The company needed to sell many of its assets to compensate for the losses coming mostly from the television division, and it needed to focus on and invest in the divisions that demonstrated the most promise. In 1992, the new management, under CEO Jorma Ollila, embarked on an intelligent course of focusing the company's strategy around telecoms and its newly found vision of "Connecting People."

The adoption of the GSM standard in 1991 opened the door for exponential growth. Already by the end of 1992, the telecom division represented 20 percent of the sales of the company. In 1993 the company's turnover grew by 500 percent, and at the height of its success Nokia was one of the world's most valuable companies, with a share price of 65 Euros, which was over forty times its value at the beginning of the 1990's and ten times more than its value today.

For Risto Siilasmaa, the founder of the successful F-Secure and a current board member of the Nokia Corporation, the great Finnish success story of all time is Nokia's rise. From a personal point of view, he believes that Nokia put Finland on the map. Up until the late 1980's, Siilasmaa did not emphasize the Finnish roots of his company Data-Fellows while doing business in the United States. By the beginning of the 1990's, Finnishness, mainly because of Nokia, became an asset for all IT companies and their professionals. Siilasmaa also admits that Nokia now poses one of the great challenges for the future of Finland. The company was and still is a leader in telecom and Internet technology innovation. However, the company's fortunes have been worsening of late, with the rise of the Apple iPhone and Samsung's Android-powered mobile devices.

I had the opportunity to work as a consultant for Nokia after writing a book on mobile marketing in 2002.[28] I was in charge of training Nokia engineers in the trends and workings of the growing mobile media business. The training was called the Nokia Mobile Media Academy. At that time, I could see that Nokia had all of the assets and the means to continue to maintain its unbelievable 40 percent market share of the world's mobile phone market. Now, as of this writing, that share has dropped to 30 percent and continues to fall.

Interestingly, Nokia had developed tactile phones as early as the year 2000. It commanded a healthy ecosystem of many hundreds of thousands of software applications developers throughout the world and, it came up, admittedly late, with Ovi, its answer to iTunes, in 2009. After the profitable rise and fall of the Symbian platform it developed a world-class platform, MeeGo, that could rival the rising dominance of Android. Despite all these strengths, Nokia still managed to lose considerable market share to Apple and Samsung.

It is simply a fact of business history that dominant corporations do not stay dominant unless they keep working harder and smarter within the right working culture at the right time. IBM missed the software turn that was capitalized upon by Microsoft. Nokia missed the opportunity to introduce its tactile phones and its enabling and entertainment platforms. Even Google has failed to take its place in the social media space taken up by Facebook. Companies rise and fall according to their use of work intelligence and by maintaining a dynamic innovative culture. For Nokia it may have been the rapid growth of a global bureaucracy that brought about a culture where out-of-the-corporate-box thinking was not encouraged or at least not so assertively promoted or acted upon. The engineering focus of the company may have blocked its development of better user design and services.

However, as we have seen in earlier chapters, Finland is a country of many historic turnarounds. Nokia itself is the product of a practically bankrupt company, which then became a technology giant in less than 10 years. As with the demise of Nortel in Canada, it may well be that this latest challenge for Finland will result in the creation of a host of highly eager and innovative companies that will produce global success stories of their own. A case in point for Finland is the gaming company Rovio and its Angry Birds, which has become the most successful digital game in history. We cover the Rovio story in Chapter 5.

3.6 Things to work on

The dark side of silence

There is a common joke in Finland about an elderly Finnish wife and her husband having some morning coffee. They have been married for over 30 years and silence has been a part of their morning routine for a while. One morning, the wife daringly breaks the silence and says to her husband, "Pekka, you haven't told me that you love me in a long time." Pekka calmly sets his coffee cup back on its plate and says: "Sirpa, I told you 30 years ago that I did. As soon as things change I will let you know." Of course, this story is an exaggeration. However, it does hold a grain of truth.

The minimalistic yet sometimes amusing communications style of Finns is well captured in the celebrated films of Aki Kaurismäki. I remember seeing one of his first films while I was studying in Paris in the end of the 80's. I was

interested in Finland because I had just been offered an exciting summer job there via a Finnish-Canadian exchange. I took some of my Canadian friends with me to see *Shadows in Paradise,* one of the early Kaurismäki films. Quite quickly, the only humor my friends could see was that silly André decided to spend his whole summer with a lot of communicatively-challenged people. Again, Kaurismäki's films portray in many ways a caricature of the people he is filming. As mentioned earlier in this chapter, silence can be a blessing. Taken to extremes, though, it can be a curse.

In my interview with Martin Saarikangas, the former CEO of Masa Yards, he stated that one of the least productive features of the Finnish personality is that Finns are often too keen on working alone. They prefer to work hard on their own and minimize their obligations to communicate. Saarikangas said that he was taught by a great Finnish professor who trained him early that a good engineer was a lazy engineer. This meant a good engineer did not attempt to reinvent the wheel. She consulted and communicated regularly with colleagues to make sure she could work in the most efficient way possible. Despite the indisputable wisdom of such advice, Finns by and large have relative difficulties working in groups.

Following the disappointing results for Finland at the Vancouver Winter Olympic Games, a special committee was formed to forge a new strategy for elite sport in Finland. The report was enlightening in many respects but one clear point to come out of its conclusions was that sports federations and other sports organizations did very little in terms of communicating best practices and pooling resources that could serve them more efficiently.

A recent business study called "Travel Guide" was conducted by Saku Tuominen and Risto Kuulasmaa: it described the barriers faced by small innovative companies wanting to expand internationally. In the study, the authors conclude that the Finnish reserve and the national shortcomings in communications with others, especially with foreigners, is one of the most important barriers to the internationalization of Finnish innovations.[29]

The right working focus

Finland's triumphs in industrialization, education, research and technology have forged a double-edged sword. Like the virtues of silence that may ultimately stifle the communication needed for success, an undue business focus on technology and products has made many companies in Finland and elsewhere miss out on significant opportunities.

IBM's belief in the 1970's that hardware would be the focus of personal computing made it sacrifice a gargantuan opportunity to software start-ups like Microsoft. European teleoperators had all of the necessary resources to come up with a Google-type service at the end of the 1990's, but they could not let go of their prevailing business models of pay-for-access. As we have seen, Nokia's belief that tactile phones did not have sufficient market acceptance caused it to lose a momentous opportunity to Apple. Similarly, Google's focus on its search and key-word marketing business completely missed the social media turn in the market, giving Facebook and other players the space to take over a good part of the mind share of Internet users.

Indeed, research in business development and innovation indicates that most of the investment made by companies in

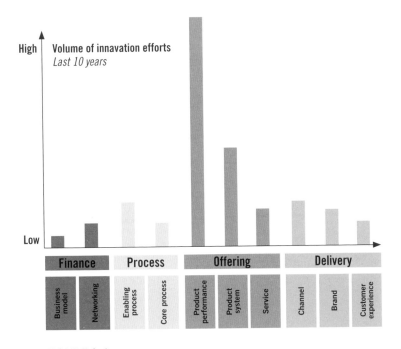

FIGURE 3-4

Source: The Doblin analysis 2005

innovation focuses on the offering of products and services. In particular, Figure 3-4 shows that the effort invested in developing the performance of current products is a particular focus of most companies over time. However, we see in Figure 3-5 that most of the value generated by companies over time comes from elsewhere. Financial innovations, such as new business models and networking, generate almost 90 percent of the value in companies over time. Google's new business model for advertising was a quantum leap for the marketing industry. Nokia's and Toyota's network of partners and sub-contractors, applying principles of just-in-time processes, are at the core of the value of these companies.

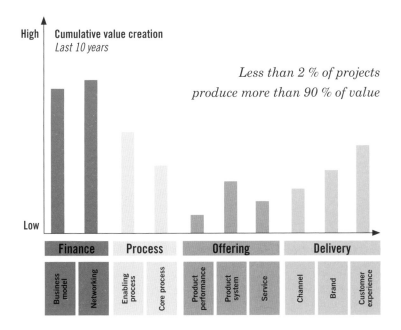

High — Cumulative value creation
Last 10 years

Less than 2 % of projects
produce more than 90 % of value

Low

Finance	Process	Offering	Delivery

Business model | Networking | Enabling process | Core process | Product performance | Product system | Service | Channel | Brand | Customer experience

FIGURE 3-5
Source: The Doblin analysis 2005

They represent much greater value than any of the individual improvements made to their products' feature set.

I personally learned my lesson on the correct locus of corporate value when I was hired as the CEO of a Finnish technology start-up called Mobicus. My colleagues Juho-Pekka Virolainen and Väinö Leskinen founded the company at the height of the Internet bubble in early 2000. We had just managed to get the last bit of venture capital available in Finland before the bubble burst. Many of our potential competitors and customers were still flush with venture cash collected when everyone believed that the Internet would transform humanity and that the growth for the mobile business would never cease. We got one million Euros of funding in our first round. Our competitors had almost all received between 10 and 20 million Euros in funding one or two years before.

My priority for Mobicus was to develop a very focused strategy and rapidly secure new partners and funding. We succeeded in this and quickly became the player with the most installations of our marketing software in the teleoperator segment. Our competitors spread their loose money around on things the market was not ready to accept. They started to fail and many of them went bankrupt. We spotted a company in the UK called Enpocket, which was working on a new business model as a mobile marketing broker for leading consumer brands. They decided to use our technology and later, when our investors left the venture capital business, Enpocket then bought Mobicus outright. In 2007, Nokia bought Enpocket and its Mobicus-developed technology for 100 million Euros. Most of this value was paid not because of our superior technology and feature set but because of the new model Enpocket had developed for marketing global brands over mobile. At the time their customer list was impressive. Unfortunately, within Nokia, a technology-driven company with many competing priorities, the Enpocket offering dried up and was terminated.

From the perspective of work utility, the Finnish Mobicus project was relatively successful. A lot of hard work, smart technology and an honest business culture helped us compete against entities much better-financed than we were. However, most of the value from this story came to the shareholders of Enpocket. This is a company that focused on developing a genuinely new business model and it was rewarded accordingly. Interestingly, once such a company was absorbed by a word-class technology and feature-enhancing company like Nokia, the potential benefits of a new way of generating income did not get prioritized. I believe that many Finnish companies large and small make similar mistakes by focusing solely on products and technology and forgetting about the customer and the market trends that may lead them to a quantum leap in value creation.

CHAPTER 4:
Sisu

Life shrinks and expands in proportion to one's courage.

Anaïs Nin

4.1 *Sisu* and success

Fear and lack of perseverance are common enemies of success. At every stage of any venture, they can make your ascent up the Possibility Model a short one. At this higher level of your climb towards success, the winds of fear and potential disappointment begin to blow stronger. Even after keeping your mind open, taking all the necessary risks and working hard and smart, the difference between success and failure often resides in your tenacity and courage. In almost any demanding endeavor your will to succeed must hold a tight grip on your undertaking to allow you to go the extra distance and reach the summit of achievement.

If Chapter 2 on trial and error was about mustering enough courage to try something new, this chapter is about the courage and persistence you need to bring about transformational change, taking it all the way to a successful conclusion.

A distinctive part of Finnish culture brings together many of the elements you need to run that extra mile towards your goal. This trait of Finnish character or, as some would say, this part of the Finnish soul, is called *sisu*. It is hard to propose a single definition or translation of this term since it has, even for Finns, a wide range of meanings depending on the context and the person. *Sisu* can best be described as a strong blend of courage and persistence; a sense of determination that is indifferent to the costs or consequences; a source of mental and spiritual strength that sometimes falls on the side of obstinacy; it is perseverance in action and a stoic and cool display of raw willpower.

Jean Sibelius, the famous Finnish composer, defined *sisu* as a metaphysical shot in the arm which makes someone do the impossible. Paavo Nurmi defined *sisu* as the dispassionate patience and strong will that comes to people miraculously in times of stress.[1] In sum, with *sisu*, most Finns have inherited a special mixture of guts and resilience, which surfaces especially when the going gets tough.

Finns have certainly had the opportunity to cultivate this remarkable psychological feature throughout their history. The list of major Finnish challenges over the past 150 years is impressive: from the great famine of the 19th century to a very violent civil war, then two wars against the USSR, one short war with Germany and one very bad economic recession in the early 1990's. If you add the smaller yet recurrent issues of long, freezing, dark winters on a lonely and isolated farm you get a sense of where *sisu* comes from.

I believe that this is a fundamental asset in the mindset of Finns which has often supported them in their numerous collective trials. *Sisu* is, however, a dangerous two-sided coin that can also pose barriers to success. We will look at this darker side of *sisu* later in the chapter.

From the perspective of the Possibility Model, a good metaphor to describe *sisu* is a circus tightrope extending from the steep cliff of the Possibility Model. At the point of departure, you are in a relatively safe status quo position. If you stay there you basically stagnate and do and learn very little. On the other side of the tightrope is a point of transformation, a dramatic change from your current position. The empowering element you need in order to get from a point of stagnation to your goal of transformation is *sisu*: a good dose of cool courage, patience and persistence that will carry you to the other side in one piece.

The transformation is not so much the new physical position at the other end of the tightrope. The change occurs all along your nerve-racking sky walk. When you reach the other end, you are indeed personally transformed by the

FIGURE 4-1: *Sisu* and transformation: The *sisu* tightrope

experience. As Bill Gates would put it, the journey is the reward and not the destination. In the context of this *sisu* tightrope, we can say the walk is in fact the transformation. The tightrope stride towards change and transformation, powered by *sisu*, is depicted in Figure 4-1.

Sisu demands an incredible disposition of the mind to make the impossible possible. What many casual observers of Finns and Finland may describe as stubbornness, close-mindedness and an unpleasant propensity for working alone is sometimes just a Finnish display of courageous single-mindedness that has seized a virtuous and improbable outcome as a focus. As mentioned previously, Finns have had many occasions to use their *sisu* and bring about major transformations of their collective fate. We present some of these exceptional times of Finnish history in the next section.

4.2 *Sisu* at war

Finnish history is rife with courageous belief in the improbable. From the country's creation in 1917 to today's peaceful and wealthy egalitarian state, Finland has undergone many major transformations. All of them have produced admirable displays of *sisu* and a resilient desire to maintain and develop the country's independence and to build a prosperous Western-style democracy.

The most extreme cases of Finnish *sisu* and transformation have involved armed conflict. The first was the civil war of 1918, which followed the country's 1917 declaration of independence. Twenty years later came a series of three more harsh wars, each running swiftly into the next: the Winter War of 1939, the Continuation War of 1941 and the Lapland war against Nazi Germany which started in 1944.

It is interesting to note that a key figure in all four wars was one exceptional Finnish leader: Marshall Carl Gustaf Emil Mannerheim. In many ways, his persona represents the positive attributes of Finnishness and *sisu*. We take a closer look at these events in the coming subsections.

The passage to statehood

Finland's birth in 1917 was its first display of *sisu*. Finns passed from Swedish to Russian rule in 1809 and thus became subjects of the Tsar of Russia. The territory of Finland became a Grand Duchy of the Russian empire. For most of the period of Russian rule, Finns were given the opportunity to develop many important independent institutions. The country enjoyed relative autonomy with its own parliament or Senate, its own currency and the reinforcement of the status of the Finnish language. It is not clear that Finland would have developed this positive autonomy had it remained a part of Sweden. The thinking behind Russia's apparently generous policy was to encourage Finnishness. This, it was hoped, would keep the country separate from its former Swedish sovereign and develop a productive economic area for the benefit of the entire Russian empire.

Throughout the 19th century a nationalistic movement called Fennomania, from the latin word Fennia which means Finland, diligently pushed for greater recognition and promotion of Finnish culture. Towards the end of the 19th century and the beginning of the 20th century the movement became stronger, especially in the wake of the harder line adopted by the Russian empire and some unfortunate attempts to "Russify" the Grand Duchy of Finland. These attempts encountered relatively disorganized but persistent resistance.

The real opportunity for Finland came with the First World War and the subsequent rise of the revolutionary Russian

Bolsheviks. Even the Finns who may have been loyal to the Tsar and to the Russian empire until that time were now eager to protect their own Finnish territory from the emerging communist revolution. Shortly after the courageous declaration of independence of 6 December 1917, the country fell into chaos, similar to the convulsions that engulfed the Russian empire itself.

The Finns' bloody civil war would start in early 1918. It lasted only three and a half months but claimed close to 40 000 lives. As in the crumbling Russian empire, the country was staunchly divided between the White bourgeois forces and the Red communist protagonists. The major and fateful defining difference for Finland, as opposed to its former Russian sovereign, is that the Whites won the war. Many of the Finns I interviewed for this book consider the violence of the civil war to be one of the country's great social failures.

For the former Finnish officers of the Tsar's army such as C.G.E. Mannerheim, the trip back to Finland in the middle of the Bolshevik revolution was like walking on a very dangerous *sisu* tightrope. As former members of the Russian imperial army, they were slated to be shot on sight throughout the Russian territory. In Helsinki, a city being taken by the Reds, their lives were also in danger.

Veijo Meri recounts a nerve-racking standoff between Mannerheim and the revolutionary Bolshevik Russian soldiers on his long train trip from his Russian military post in Odessa to Helsinki in late 1917.[2] In an impressive display of self-control and fearless confrontation, Mannerheim leveled a frozen yet penetrating stare at the Bolshevik soldiers and explained that he was a Finnish citizen on his way home. Had he flinched or started to fight, he would have been shot instantly. This kind of control of one's nerves under pressure is one of the impressive features of Finnish *sisu*. If the Bolsheviks had killed Mannerheim or other key Finnish officers of the Imperial army, the impact on the outcome of the Finnish civil war could have been considerable.

The south of the country, including Helsinki, was in the hands of the Reds. The west and center of the country were under White control. Through Mannerheim's leadership as the general of the White army, the embryonic Finnish state was able to secure its independence from the communist influence of the nascent Soviet Union. The White army was mostly made up of Finnish soldiers who trained in Germany during the First World War, and who landed back in Finland through the port of Vaasa. They received the assistance of the German army, which joined in fighting the communists and helping in the struggle to take back Red-controlled Helsinki. All of this came at a heavy human cost, but the enduring dream of Fennomania was born and Finland was transformed from a vassal province into an internationally recognized independent state.

Defending and unifying the state

If in 1917 some had believed the creation of a lasting independent Finnish state to be improbable, the notion of tiny Finland defeating the colossal Soviet Union some twenty years later was even more extraordinary–close to a human miracle. The use of the word *sisu* is perhaps most deeply associated with this critical part of Finnish history.

At the beginning of World War II, Germany and the USSR made a pact by which Finland would fall within the Soviet sphere of influence. The Soviets began to exercise their influence over Finland by making demands for Finnish territory. In the intensive negotiations prior to the armed conflict between the two nations, the Soviets made what they may have believed to be a reasonable offer to Finland.

The Soviets requested that most of the southeast territory of Finland (Karelia) be annexed to the Soviet Union and that the southern port of Hanko be surrendered to Soviet control. In return, the Soviet Union claimed to be willing to bequeath significant northern Soviet territories to Finland. The Soviet Union was eager to create a greater territorial buffer around the city of Leningrad (today's St. Petersburg) and a better point of control and access to the Baltic Sea from the port of Hanko. The Finnish representatives courageously said that they could not accept this offer.

Stalin was surprised by the stubbornness and perhaps the courageous *sisu* of his Finnish counterparts. The refusal of the Finns can be explained by the fact that few in Finland believed the Soviets would continue to respect Finnish state sovereignty if the deal's terms were accepted. This suspicion would prove to be accurate in relation to similar Soviet demands made on Estonia, Latvia and Lithuania. An acceptance of the Soviet terms would have given the USSR a foothold for taking control of Finland, as indeed the Soviets later took control of most of Eastern Europe.

The cost of the Finnish refusal would be the bloody confrontations in the Winter War of 1939 and then again in the Continuation War of 1941. The Finns certainly chose the riskiest and most unpredictable path to maintain their place as an established and independent nation in the international community.

In late November 1939, the Soviet Army began invading Finland. Mannerheim, following up his roles as the victorious general of the White army and as the second Regent of the young Finnish state, became commander-in-chief of the Finnish army. He received the unique title of Marshall Mannerheim. Finns had already started devising defense plans, despite some resistance from certain government members who still believed in the possibility of a peaceful resolution.

Asking for help

During this time, it is interesting to note that Finland made a plea to the United States for financial and military assistance. A group called Friends of Finland produced a compelling public relations film called "Finland Fights" at the onset of the Winter War.[3] The film features Jean Sibelius and his music as well as a touching plea for help from the well-known Paavo Nurmi in white Winter War camouflage gear, with the Finnish and American flags in the background. The film appealed to common values of democracy and religion that were being violated by a "godless" communist aggressor. The film also contains former US President Herbert Hoover's strong support for the Finnish cause and the Finland Relief Fund Inc. Though this Finnish media campaign produced a lot of American sympathy, it was clear that Finland would never receive American military assistance in its war against the Soviets.

Mannerheim established his war headquarters in the City of Mikkeli. In a startling confrontation between an emerging superpower and a small independent country, the Finns, without any foreign military assistance, were able to keep the Soviet army from taking hold of their country. This display of raw *sisu* cost the Finnish army over 20 000 lives.

The Finnish winter was an important ally for the young country's brave soldiers. They fought an innovative type of warfare, a precursor of modern guerrilla battle techniques, putting the soldiers on skis and taking advantage of forest cover and white camouflage suits so they could emerge from the trees and the snow in swift, unexpected attacks. The Finnish methods effectively slowed down a much larger yet ill-equipped Soviet force in the depths of a harsh winter.

This short but intense war was followed by a brief period of peace. Tension was still high between Finland and the Soviet Union. It became clear for Finns that France and England would align themselves with the Soviet Union in their strategy to defeat Germany. In addition, when Germany invaded Denmark and Norway, any Finnish hope of receiving help from the West was literally cut off.

A new strategy

Given this state of affairs, Marshall Mannerheim and the new Finnish President Risto Ryti began to forge a new war strategy based on an alliance with the sole force that could give them a chance in keeping the Soviets at bay: Germany. This was perceived to be the only way to survive another likely confrontation with the Soviet Union. During the short period of peace, over 70 Finnish army officers secretly visited Germany while in turn many German emissaries and army agents visited Finland. Finally, in May 1941, the high military commands of Germany and Finland agreed in Salzburg on joint military operations.

In June of that year Hitler broke his pact with Stalin and launched his massive attack against the Soviet Union--Operation Barbarossa. The new offensive included German forces deployed in Finnish Lapland. On the same day, Finland was back at war with the Soviet Union. This time it was fighting as an ally of Germany. It was an effective yet uneasy alliance.

Mannerheim himself was not personally very fond of Germany despite the importance of the help he received from that country during the civil war and again during the Continuation War. As an officer of the Tsar's Imperial Army he had been at war against Austria, Germany and Hungary during World War I. In that war he bravely fought the Austrian army on the Polish front, and was honored as an important general of the Russian Imperial army.

Given his personal experiences, Mannerheim was careful, throughout his Continuation War military campaigns, not to go too far and aggravate his Soviet adversaries. He refused, for example, to attack Leningrad at a time when the war momentum would have made it possible. Indeed for most Finnish military officers and politicians, the war was all about winning a solid yet respectable peace with the Soviets, one that would ensure the country's continued autonomy. It is important to note here that the Finnish government never emulated or participated in Germany's systematic persecution of Jewish and other minorities during the time of their military alliance.

Paradoxically, Hitler greatly admired Mannerheim. He saw in him a superior officer and war strategist. Another fascinating war film from that period is a German-produced propaganda film about the surprise visit Hitler made on the occasion of Mannerheim's 75th birthday, in early June 1942. This was Hitler's only visit to Finland and underscores the importance he gave to Mannerheim and to the German military alliance with the Finns. Mannerheim made a reciprocal visit to Hitler only a month later. This sent a strong and perhaps distorted signal to the West that Finland was growing even closer to Germany. In fact, Mannerheim kept his relationship with the German army civilized but not cordial. His goal was an honorable resolution with the Soviets, not an unrealistic decisive military victory over a country with more than 7 times the number of soldiers as there were Finnish citizens.

This complex set of diplomatic and military circumstances, and the resulting delicate position of the military and political leaders of Finland during this period, emphasizes one of the most interesting features of *sisu*. This is the disposition of the mind to do anything that needs to be done in order to achieve your goal. To the outside world, it may have seemed irrational and even hypocritical to first appeal for help to the United States by stressing Finnish democratic values, and then shortly thereafter form an alliance with one of the worst tyrants in human history. Ironically, at the end of the war Finns had to fight their former Germans allies and push them out of Finnish Lapland after peace terms were made with the Soviet Union in 1944. This succeed-at-all costs aspect of *sisu* is both a little bit Machiavellian and obstinate in the conviction that the end can justify the means.

Despite the ambiguity of the Finnish position throughout the period of the Second World War, the international reputation of the Finns was largely favorable. Mannerheim was a world-renowned celebrity, especially in neutral yet cosmopolitan Switzerland, where he enjoyed spending his free time even during the war. I remember discussing this part of Finnish history with a friend of our family who was a soldier in the French Resistance. He told me that, despite their ultimate alliance with Germany, the Finns were an inspiration for all of his comrades fighting for a free France. He said: "Oh those Finns. They are a brave nation. When we were losing hope, we thought of them bravely fighting ten against one and it gave us strength."

The heavy price of freedom

In these armed conflicts with the Soviet Union, the initial size of the Finnish army was approximately 350 000 soldiers. At the height of the Continuation War, the Soviets had over one million soldiers at the Finnish border. By the end of both wars, over 90 000 Finnish soldiers had lost their lives. The military losses on the Soviet side are estimated to be a much heavier, at 400 000 soldiers.[4] This a ratio of nearly 5-to-1: five Soviet military fatalities for each Finnish one. The ratio stands as a famous measure of Finnish *sisu*. Indeed, many Finns regard it as one of the most important Finnish Miracles since the country became independent.

Probably the best-known book about this inspiring event in Finnish history is *The Unknown Soldier* by Väinö Linna. The novel, which has twice been turned into a movie, offers a ground-level view of ordinary Finnish soldiers fighting what sometimes felt like an impossible war. Their story is perhaps the one most Finns associate with the word *sisu* even today.

The overwhelming size and strength of the Soviet Union made it overconfident at the Winter War's beginning. The Soviets assumed that Finland would easily be annexed to its sphere of influence. Some of the first Soviet officers to lose their lives in war are said to have possessed ready-made invitations to the celebration for the Soviet victory, set to be held at the old Russian Governor's House in Helsinki. In this context, you can conclude that Finland bravely played its cards right in using Nazi assistance, and was fortunate not to have faced the mighty Soviet Union on its own. All in all, over 10 million Soviet soldiers and 10 million Soviet civilians lost their lives during the Second World War.

This *realpolitik* is something Finns understood very well when developing their peace and cooperation initiatives with the Soviet Union during the Cold War. Because of the nation's eventful and challenging political history, Finland has always had a rich diversity of political parties representing the full range of the political spectrum. Extreme socialists and right-wing conservatives have sat side by side in the Finnish parliament since the country's inception. One positive political outcome of the Winter and Continuation Wars was a greater sense of national unity, built around the quasi-unanimous desire to keep Finland independent. This is perhaps another minor Finnish Miracle because it has forced hardliners from all parties to continuously compromise and work constructively together to build a strong and independent nation.

A Miraculous Finn
Carl Gustaf Emil
MANNER
HEIM

C.G. Mannerheim was born in Askainen, Finland in 1867 and died in Lausanne, Switzerland in 1951. He was the Finnish Republic's sixth president (1944 to 1946), its second regent (1918 to 1919) and Finland's only Marshal. The commander in chief of the Finnish army in three different wars, he was also the head of the Finnish Red Cross, and a notable explorer who for two years produced valuable maps of Central Asia. He took part in the Russo-Japanese war and led a division of 40 000 cavalrymen of the Russian army in the First World War. He was a first-class equestrian rider and hunter. He was a generator of new trends and customs, a writer and one of his generation's most cultivated and worldly men.[5]

Mannerheim epitomizes the Finnish Miracle. When scrutinized through the stages of the Possibility Model, Mannerheim did many things right to make the impossible possible in his own life and for the young Finnish state. In terms of broadmindedness he was ahead of his time. He spoke five languages and travelled extensively across Asia and Europe. He had a flexible and intelligent relationship with neighboring nations, which led him to practice either cooperation or resistance depending on the needs and interests of his fledgling nation.

With some thirty years in the service of the army of the Russian Tsar, he experienced both sacrifice and satisfaction on a long road of trial and error. On top of being a military genius, he was an astute politician. His incisive political vision allowed him to lead Finland to the optimal decisions that kept the country independent, and that avoided

CHAPTER 4 **SISU**   **173**

wasting the Finnish people's extraordinary acts of bravery and sacrifice.

An icon of *sisu*, he was fearless and, some historians have said, almost cruel in making choices that would generate dramatic political and social change. Finally, he was authentic in his ideals, and stood by his beliefs in freedom and independence to the day he died. As fate would have it, he was the right man, at the right time, in the right place to secure the growth of Finland as an independent state. Recently, a major motion picture about Mannerheim has been in development. If completed as planned, it will become the most elaborate and expensive production in the history of the Finnish film industry.

4.3 *Sisu* in business

As we discussed earlier, one of the great Finnish Miracles occurred relatively soon after the period of the Second World War. This was the colossal task of creating a new industrial base for Finland that could ensure its survival and prosperity as a nation. After the war the Finnish economy was in crisis. Despite the eminent prospect of material shortages, massive investments were made in the forestry, metal and shipbuilding industries. Factories, plants and other facilities were practically built from scratch. Impressive investments were made in education so that the new industrial Finland would have capable and innovative hands to bring the nation up to the level of the most advanced industrialized societies.

Paradoxically much of this growth was the result of the industrial capability built up to pay off the hefty war debts imposed by the Soviet Union: the debts totaled approximately 600 million dollars. In the end, this burden turned out to be a blessing and Finland emerged as one of the rare countries to pay its war debts in full.

During the 1950's the Soviet Union became the target market for almost 20 percent of all of Finland's exports. In sectors like metals and ships, that percentage reached 80 percent. As we saw in the previous chapter, this fast-growing success was fuelled by a lot of working harder and smarter in Finland.

By the 1970's, Finland was already holding its own, and much of the immigration from Finland to countries like Canada, the USA and Australia diminished significantly. In less than twenty years, Finland had passed from an agrarian state to a much more urbanized and solidly industrialized country. This was a display of *sisu* at its best: a long, painful yet unwavering road towards the goal of financial and social success despite the pressure and influence of the communist superpower living next door. It was yet another Finnish Miracle in the making.

All of this came to a rather abrupt halt towards the end of the 1980's and the beginning of the 1990's. Many Finnish companies had become complacent and unduly dependent on the system of trade and barter with the Soviet Union. Innovation declined because the level of expectations in the Soviet Union was low: the Soviets basically bought almost anything the Finns made. For obvious political reasons, Western goods were not generally available in the Soviet Union at that time.

When the Soviet Union collapsed, so did much of its trade with Finland, and there were no takers in the rest of the world for a good part of the lower-quality products the Finns were producing. This made a good number of Finnish businesses fail and created record unemployment levels of well over 20 percent in some regions. From 1986 to 1989 GDP growth was at a very healthy 4.3 percent. Following the collapse of the Soviet Union in 1990, the Finnish GDP fell by a dramatic 7.1 percent in 1991 and did not see positive numbers again until 1995.

To make things worse, Finnish banks failed because of the high risks they took in lending to companies and individuals who were not creditworthy. Worse still, the Finnish currency, the *Markka*, fell rapidly in value and a massive set of foreign loans in yen and dollars needed to be repaid at a huge premium. All of this exploded into a full-blown recession in 1991.

If there were ever a time in their recent history for Finns to display their *sisu*, this was it. From this great financial and industrial challenge, Finns rebuilt and especially re-modernized their industries. Some clearly non-competitive fields, such as the low-end textile industry, were essentially terminated. As we saw in the earlier chapter, the worst year of the Finnish recession also marked the rebirth of a more focused Nokia and the international launch of their new GSM standard phones, which produced a first-year result of 500 percent growth in company turnover. Finland joined the European Union in 1995 to enhance its access to European markets and to cheaper capital. This dramatic turnaround of the Finnish economy–which includes the rise of Nokia as one of the world's leading global technology companies–is the most recent of the country's large-scale miracles.

4.4 *Sisu* in sports

We have seen that elite athletic performances have been a defining part of the Finnish national identity. They have also constituted symbolic evidence of the pervasiveness of Finnish *sisu*. During his lifetime, Paavo Nurmi was the most successful runner and Olympian of all time. Finnish runners literally ran Finland onto the world map. Similar fame has come to Finnish cross-country skiers like Juha Mieto and Veikko Hakulinen. Mieto was the Olympic champion and dominant skier of the 1970's, while Hakulinen was the three-time Olympic champion at three different Olympics in the 1950's and 60's. Both of these strong competitors were known for their explosive displays of raw willpower.

Finnish women also showed their *sisu* in cross-country skiing with the likes of Marja-Liisa Kirvesniemi, who took three gold medals in the Sarjevo winter Olympics in 1984. Kirvesniemi and her husband Harri are one of the few couples to have competed in six separate Olympic Winter Games. Finally, Marjo Matikainen-Kallström is another successful skier from the 1980's, with a gold medal at the Calgary

Winter Olympics. Interestingly, she has been remembered for her screaming of a swear word at the 1987 World Championships in Oberstdorf. She shouted "*havuja perkele*," which in English could be translated "twigs, goddamn it!"

The word *perkele* comes from the name of a mythological Finnish god who in modern times has become equated with the Devil. It is generally used as a strong swearword in Finnish: the closest English meaning would be as a more potent version of "goddamn it." The reason Matikainen-Kallström was so adamant about her twigs was that some sticky lumps of snow were stuck under her skis because of the bad weather. She needed her support team to throw some twigs in front of her to get the lumps off. Her persistent yelling and perhaps her resort to foul language ultimately won her the gold medal in that race. Finnish *sisu* is indeed an interesting mixture of decisiveness and a do-what-it-takes attitude. It won't always win you style points but it usually gets the job done.

One of the most inspiring displays of transformational *sisu* in the history of Finnish sports was a very special 10 000 meter race by the legendary Lasse Virén at the Munich games of 1972. A young policeman from Myrskylä, Virén began his international career at the age of 22 at the European Athletics Championships in Helsinki. He placed a disappointing 7th and 17th place in the 5 000 and 10 000 meter races respectively. He then came to the Munich Summer Olympics as an underdog the following year. After some grueling altitude training in Kenya, he was in world-class form and his performance in the 10 000 meter final became one of the marvels of track-and-field.

Virén ran a solid twelve laps, but fell after becoming entangled with two other runners. Millions of Finns, glued to their black and white TV's, held their breath in horror. What happened afterwards is the stuff of legends. Lasse

Virén got to his feet and caught up with the leading pack in less than 150 meters. He then accelerated to an unbelievable pace and, despite his fall, won the race with a world-record-breaking time of 27:38:40. The whole of Finland was ecstatic and the race became a defining moment, a symbol of the nation's rise to modernity and international success. Virén was another Finnish Miracle and one of the contemporary personal icons of *sisu* because he literally transformed a catastrophe into a blazing victory.

Another notable story of intense *sisu* in sports comes from an adoptive Finn. Her name was Dominick Arduin and she was a French and Finnish endurance skier, climber and adventurer. She left her native France in 1988 to settle down in Finnish Lapland, where she trained and worked as a guide in the tourist industry for over 15 years. She lived very much like a Finn and rapidly adopted the local culture. She was a driven woman. She had grown up in the Alps and been orphaned at a very young age. She was also a cancer survivor and had become an only child after the passing of her sister.

She caught the spirit of *sisu* and grew resolute in her determination to be the first women in the world to ski to the geographic North Pole alone. In 2001, she reached the Magnetic North Pole. In 2003 she was rescued after her first failed attempt to reach the geographic North Pole. Most of her toes needed to be amputated because of frostbite.

This extreme challenge had only been accomplished by three people before her. Arduin, imbued with *sisu*, would spare no effort to see her project through to its completion. Despite the amputation of her toes, she kept on training with a prosthesis to reach her goal. She also continued to raise money, and mortgaged her own house to help fund her second attempt. There was no stopping her and she appeared several times on Finnish television, where she was asked directly if she had a death wish. She simply answered that she had *sisu* and a dream that a woman could achieve this demanding journey.

I remember having dinner with her on her last night in Helsinki before her departure for her second attempt for the North Pole. I was involved in the negotiation of her sponsorship contracts for future projects. During our dinner, she was unbelievably determined and could not imagine failure as an option. Unfortunately, climate change had made the passage to the North Pole more dangerous than ever, with ice melting and breaking more often than before. She was equipped with a raft, but it could do little to help her if the ice was to break too often and the gaps were to grow too wide. She never came back.

This was a case of *sisu* encountering a deplorable stroke of bad luck. The intensity of *sisu* usually goes hand in hand with the level of risk. The fall from the tightrope is always a possibility. But for some who uncompromisingly embrace the *sisu* vision, the thrill of the walk is well worth the risk of the fall.

4.5 The bad *sisu*

Sisu is, therefore, a powerful force within Finnish culture. It can make the impossible possible. However, it has also been known to make possible impossible. There is a dark side to *sisu*. When combined with more negative elements of human behavior such as closed-mindedness, reflexive stubbornness, narcissistic authoritarianism, alcohol abuse, and other high-risk mental states, the result can be destructive.

The dark side of *sisu*, or bad *sisu*, is called *paha sisu* in Finnish. A person who has bad *sisu* is said to be *pahansisuinen*. It is a term generally used for people who have a difficult personal nature. The mildest form of *paha sisu* in Finns is a recurrent display of stubbornness and a relatively solitary closed-mindedness that sometimes makes Finnish culture challenging to work with. This came out in the study conducted by Ben Nothnagel mentioned in Chapter one. Indeed, in this survey of 1200 members of cross border teams, Finns were perceived to be notably stubborn, with a preference to work alone and a trait of communicating less effectively with other team members from other countries.

Again, the brighter side of this feature can be found in many of the examples identified above. Stubbornness may be particularly useful when you are facing challenging stressful situations like a war, a recession or a high-level sports competition. However, in a stable working context the ability to take the time to consider other avenues of action in teams and ponder and discuss alternatives proposed by others may be more appropriate and conducive to better outcomes.

An early observation of this trickier side of *sisu* in Finnish working life comes from something the Swedes have

PERKELE!

called "management by *perkele*." Perkele, the colorful and phonetically strong Finnish swearword that we have already mentioned, was still commonly used by charismatic Finnish business leaders of the 1970's and 80's. Nokia's CEO Kari Kairamo used this word spontaneously, for instance, when he was in a difficult spot by publicly saying: "Yes, we will fix this, goddamn it!"

This way of communicating made an impression on the Swedes who, by contrast, are known for practicing the art of discussion and for respecting the right of everyone to be heard at least once before a decision is made. The old Finnish management style comes from a need to decide quickly and promote fast execution. In the rapidly industrializing post-war Finland, where experience as a military officer was seen as a necessity to access upper management positions, the management-by-*perkele* style was perhaps the optimal way to rapidly grow an industrial economy.

Today, this type of management has practically disappeared with the retirement of *patruuna* generation,[7] and the rise of new industries where workers are increasingly independent experts who react quite negatively to an authoritarian or fear-driven style of management. However, the legacy of the quick decision making and fast and effective execution is still seen as a valuable Finnish way of doing things. Some Finns call this *tekemisen meininki*, which is an expression that refers to a good and effective working groove that gets the job done well and in good time.

Applied carefully, this efficiency-driven Finnish way of working can be useful if it leaves room for the modern workplace necessity of positive and innovation-stimulating discussions with peers. It seems that this is one of the growth areas identified by many Finnish workplace environment studies. In his book on Finnish leadership, Eero Kostamo points to a study where managers were asked to make self-evaluations of their leadership skills. These were then compared to the evaluations that employees made of the managers' leadership skills. The biggest discrepancy appeared in the area of general manager-employee cooperation. This kind of finding signals the potential need to improve, to some degree, the Finnish employee ownership and involvement in decision-making processes.[8]

The sisu of the True Finns

One recent Finnish success at home has caught the eye of the international press. It is the victory at the last general elections of the True Finns party. At the election in April 2011, the party received 19.1 percent of the popular vote, making it four times more popular than it was in the previous election, when it received only 4.9 percent of the vote. This caused a minor revolution in Finnish politics. For the past few decades the three main parties of the right, the center and the left have regularly and uneventfully shared power among themselves, typically leaving one party of this political triumvirate out of government for a term or two.

Much of the international media coverage of the True Finns' victory was not very positive. The image of the True Finns presented abroad was one of an extreme right-wing xenophobic party. Having little information on the real nature of the background and political agenda of the party, many international media sources simply assumed that this emerging political entity resembled the extremist parties of Jean-Marie Le Pen's Front National of France or Jörg Haider's Freedom Party of Austria. This is, however, an exceptionally misleading comparison.

The True Finns party has a clear socialist ideology and is supportive, as almost all Finnish political parties are, of the welfare state. In the Finnish Parliament, the members of the party sit in the central left position. The rest of the political program of the party can be described as rightwing in that it promotes traditional family values and nationalism. The party is also known for its restrictive policy on immigration. Certain members of the party have indeed used some xenophobic rhetoric in public. It is important to note that the leader of the party, Timo Soini, has emphasized that the party is not xenophobic. He has justified the immigration policy of the party on protectionist social and economic grounds. As opposed to the extreme rightwing leaders of Europe, Soini is a supporter of the state of Israel.

The real driving force behind the success of the True Finns is rooted in the common folk's fear of losing sovereignty or access to welfare in the face of an increasingly interconnected and globalised world. The victory of the party was mainly fueled by an appeal to ordinary people's concerns and anxieties about the seemingly perpetual need to help economically challenged countries of the EU such as Greece and Portugal, and the increasing pressure to take in refugees from troubled areas of the world. This type of anti-EU or protectionist political group can be found, at least to some degree, in almost all EU states today.

Timo Soini is the main figurehead of the True Finns Party. He was instrumental in creating it 16 years ago. The party traces its ideological roots to the Rural Party, founded in the 1950's by the charismatic Veikko Vennamo. The Rural Party had broken away from the party of the Agrarian League (later to become the Center Party), led by Urho Kekkonen. Vennamo was a populist politician, famous for his political catchphrase "*kansa tietää*" which means "the people know." The best performances of the Rural Party were in the 1970's and 1980's, when they took 10 percent of the popular national vote. The True Finns were a very small party in the early years of their establishment. At the general election of 1999, the party received only one percent of the vote. In twelve years, the popularity of the party has grown twenty-fold. On victory night in April, Timo Soini, in his habitual colorful language, came up with a new catchphrase to capture the way he and his party had transformed Finnish politics: "Nyt tuli iso jytky!" which means that "now a big bang has come!"

The party has changed its name in English to The Finns. The name True Finns was actually a misnomer of sorts, a good example of what is sometimes lost in translation. The better translation of *perussuoma-lainen* would be the Basic Finns. Basic Finns, like many "basic" citizens around the world, have a hard time expressing solidarity in challenging economic times.

This is most likely not the best strategy to develop sustainable trust and assistance from other countries or improve your national image, but it is certainly a common human feature in many countries, and certainly shouldn't be exaggerated or demonized per se.

Timo Soini was interviewed for this book.[9] Soini himself is a relatively spiritual man who is paradoxically a Catholic, as opposed to the vast majority of "basic" Finns who are Lutheran. Though he has made it a point to emphasize his non-racist motives for his tight immigration policy, a few notorious figures in the party have unfortunately not been as tolerant.

Though the ideology of the True Finns and Timo Soini may, on its surface, be at odds with the precepts of success presented in this book, their story is not without interest. Regardless of your political or ideological convictions, you have to recognize that Timo Soini is, in his own rustic way, an example of some of the positive sides of *sisu* and Finnishness. He is an articulate and knowledgeable man and thus has had the required open-mindedness to optimally assess his political opportunities. He took considerable political risks by not joining any of the mainstream parties and by participating in the creation of a new and unknown party. He worked hard and made some intelligent decisions on the positioning of this party. He stubbornly believed in his ability to win a good part of the electorate for a period of 16 years until he achieved his desired transformation in 2011.

Finally and perhaps most importantly, it is his authenticity that won the hearts and minds of his people. With Soini, as with many Finns, what you see is what you get: total Finnish simplicity from a man who makes little effort to make things look better than they are, including his own personal image. He exudes Finnish frankness with a twist of good wit and a non-arrogant flavor of self-confidence that most "basic" Finns can easily relate to.

Sisu and bad spirits

In spite of its stellar record on education, well-being and global competitiveness, Finland is not without its share of social challenges. From alcoholism to personal violence to suicide, Finland definitely has a challenge in containing its special set of recurring social problems. The darker side of the Finnish soul is a delicate subject.

From the perspective of this particular stage of the Possibility Model, one could say that the more negative aspects of Finnish culture are examples of bad *sisu* that can abruptly stop your journey to success and easily make the possible impossible. From the perspective of the theme of this book, you can perhaps surmise that given the pervasiveness of some of the Finnish social problems, one of the Finnish Miracles is that Finland is indeed a stellar success in light of its social challenges.

The dark side of Finnishness is such a vast subject that it can't possibly be covered adequately here. We can, however, glimpse its frightening dimensions by taking a brief look at one very taboo area of Finnish life: the relationship of many Finns to alcohol.

Statistically the total consumption of alcohol in Finland does not seem to be significantly higher per capita than in other European countries. According to certain statistics from the World Health Organisation (the WHO), the consumption of alcohol per capita in Finland is only slightly higher than the European average. Finns consume about the same amount as Germans, but less than people in Ireland or Portugal. Per capita consumption is, however, higher than in most English-speaking countries (USA, Australia, Canada and New Zealand) and a little higher that in the other Nordic countries.[10]

One distinctive quality of Finnish drinking patterns is that they are oddly and often unevenly distributed. A minority of Finns are, for instance, responsible for the lion's share of national alcohol consumption. In 2010, the annual alcohol consumption had risen to ten liters of pure alcohol per inhabitant. The National Agency of Health (STAKES) has published statistics according to which ten percent of the population is responsible for almost 50 percent of all alcohol consumed in the country. This means that every tenth Finn drinks approximately fifty liters of pure alcohol per year. This figure is somewhat disturbing because, at these levels, you can assume that almost every tenth Finn has some kind of issue with alcohol.

Finnish industrialization, urbanization and increased personal wealth have partly contributed to the considerable increase in alcohol consumption over the past four decades. This has been compounded by lower price levels resulting from the relatively recent reduction of alcohol taxes and the free movement of alcohol products within the EU.

Another interesting aspect of Finnish drinking culture is that many Finns drink in peaks and troughs rather than on a moderate and regular basis. The continental European habit of drinking wine with a meal on a daily basis is generally quite alien to Finnish culture. For many Finns, still today, drinking alcohol is more of a weekend pastime, a companion for your weekly sauna session or simply a way of getting drunk.

Drinking to get drunk is surprisingly common and accepted. In 1968 about 14 percent of men drank "in earnest" at least once a month. In 1984, the corresponding figure had risen to 26 percent and has stayed more or less the same since then. Drinking to get drunk is rarer among women than men, but the relative rate of increase has been greater. In 1968, about one percent of women reported they had been drunk at least once a month. That number increased to eight percent in 1992 and has remained at the same level ever since.[11]

All of these excesses naturally take their toll on national health and well-being. The direct social costs of alcohol abuse in Finland are estimated to be around 1 billion Euros per year. Finns are not alone in facing this problem since this sinister figure is 30 billion Euros at the EU level. In 2005, alcohol diseases and poisonings were the most common causes of death among working age people. In 2007, 3097 people died of alcohol abuse. The list of other direct social challenges related to alcohol is unfortunately long: liver and other cancers, traffic accidents, family and relationship problems, workplace problems, unrest in public places, suicide, violence and crime.

From a Finnish cultural perspective, the combination of *sisu* and too much alcohol can indeed be a lethal mix. Large quantities of alcohol quickly absorbed can release a spree of very bad and misplaced *sisu*, causing substantial personal and material losses. The majority of both the perpetrators and the victims of violent crime in Finland are under the influence of alcohol during the act. Statistics show that in homicides the share of perpetrators inebriated during the act was 61 to 75 percent. In attempted homicides the figure is 71 to 78 percent, and in assaults 71 to 73 percent. During the last two decades the number of inebriated offenders has increased. Roughly half of Finnish crimes of theft involve the use of alcohol.[12]

Despite these gloomy figures, there are some redeeming aspects to Finnish drinking habits. As indicated above, the excesses of Finnish drinking are concentrated among a minority of Finns and generally appear in a limited number of circumstances. By and large, moderate and recreational drinking in Finland is a fairly positive driver of socialization and business networking. Typically shy and silent, Finns tend to open up significantly once they have had a few relaxing drinks. This is often the only way to have a better idea of what your Finnish friend or colleague is really thinking.

In the work-hard-and-play-hard attitude that Finns adapted in their years of rapid industrialization, the play-hard element has often used alcohol as its great facilitator. Many famous heads of leading Finnish companies have been known for their excesses in this area. What is somewhat impressive is the will and ability of many Finns to show up at work even after a fairly hard bout of recreational drinking in an interesting morning display of Finnish *sisu* and the superb Lutheran work ethic.

Many older Finnish *patruuna* have confided in me that much of the old trade successes with the former Soviet Union and Russia were fueled by leveraging their common drinking culture. Their stories tell of delegations of Swedes and Brits who would refuse to drink all of the vodka on offer or even worse try to fake it by pouring some of it in a plant or a cup. These behaviors, they say, were ultimate signs of weakness and suspicion in a Russian host's eyes and an excellent reason to stop negotiations and sign more deals with their Finnish peers, who had a better stomach for hard and honest drinking. I am sure that these stories carry an element of urban and industrial myth, but given my experience with these cultures I expect that they hold a grain of truth.

One of the more recent and positive elements of the Finnish relationship with alcohol is the growing ability of Finns to talk about the issue more openly. Consider the public discussions and media coverage that followed the brilliant Finnish victory in the 2011 World Ice Hockey

Championships. In the heat of the celebrations a few of the Finnish team members visibly had a few too many. Most of them were loose and happy but clearly in control of their speech and movements. For some in Finland and abroad, this was a display of shameful behavior. For others, it was an understandable and accepted way of celebrating a much-coveted world title. In any event, the public discussion in TV shows, newspapers and blogs was particularly profuse.

In this way, Finland has come a long way–from avoiding any mention of alcoholism to tackling a complex social and cultural phenomenon in an open and public fashion. This heightened degree of open-mindedness is, as we have seen, the beginning of any journey towards finding successful solutions to difficult problems.

Another sign of the evolution in the public debate about the use of alcohol can be seen in the blockbuster-like success of the books of Juha Vuorinen. Vuorinen is by now the most successful Finnish-language author in the country. His books have sold over one million copies domestically over the past 12 years. This is a quantum leap from the meager "gold standard" of 20 000 copies needed to be considered a very successful Finnish writer.

Vuorinen's books are about a poor soul tormented by his addiction to alcohol. His debut book was called *A Crazy Drunk's Diary* and was an instant smash. In the late 1990's his book drafts were completely rejected by most publishers and the writers' guild of Finland. The country's intelligentsia was seemingly not ready for this kind of crass and humorous depiction of an alcoholic lifestyle. His unmatched commercial success has proven these gatekeepers wrong.

Many criticize Vuorinen for condoning this kind of behavior and making a celebrated hero out of a drunk. Others see this as a positive and cathartic social exercise that puts the issue directly at the center of a public forum, providing a platform for an open and constructive debate around the use of alcohol. Indeed, sometimes the best therapy comes from looking at yourself in the mirror and having a good laugh.

My personal good laugh on this subject comes every year when I try to book a visiting Santa Claus on Christmas Eve for my children. The list of prospective Santas is long in the classified section in December, but it is quite difficult to differentiate between them on the basis of their ads. They ALL market themselves as "Sober Santas." None claims to be a "singing Santa" or an "experienced Santa." No, the best Santa is a sober Santa. The rest, it seems, is simply a nice bonus.

The same all-important qualifier permeates the personal ad sections. Almost every male description on a dating service will have an allusion to sobriety. Over twenty years ago, I used to sing on the market squares in Helsinki. I ended up making most of my money not necessarily for my singing skills but for my theatrical improvisations around the constant flow of visibly drunken hobos who frequently tried to interrupt my performances. The resulting mix of laughs and shame in my Finnish audience made me a relatively wealthy visiting student.

Finland's relationship to alcohol has definitely been a complex social cross to bear. This is where Finnish *sisu* clearly needs to exercise its mystical magic in the future.

Sisu of shame

The Finnish language has a vivid expression to describe the power of *sisu* in making the impossible possible. This expression is "*menee vaikka läpi harmaan kiveen.*" This translates into "*to go through even grey granite if needed.*" The strong image captures the two sides of *sisu*. On the one hand, it describes the great energy and almost blind determination *sisu* generates in making the impossible possible. The imagery is similar to the expression "moving mountains" in English.

The metaphor is inspiring because it creates a positive mental disposition to confront a seemingly unfeasible task. But the expression also reveals the somewhat irrational, absurdly stubborn and succeed-at-all-costs aspect of the term. *Sisu* sometimes need to be taken with a bit of skepticism and commonsense or you might just end up breaking your skull against that granite for nothing.

Sisu, in addition, can sometimes cross over to the side of the irrational and the immoral when it is taken too far. One case of *sisu* that has clearly driven some good Finns towards immoral pursuits is the unfortunate story of the Cross-Country Skiing World Championships in Lahti in 2001.

To fully understand the nature and impact of this sad Finnish story you must place it in its historical context. In the summer of 1998 the world of cycling was shaken by a large-scale doping scandal. The *Tour de France* organization and the International Cycling Union (ICU) were under pressure from a very public doping scandal. The media went on to blaming the leaders of world sports for their loose efforts in combating the general and ever-growing issue of doping in elite athletic events. Governments and international sports organizations fell under public pressure to do something credible and decisive in the fight against doping. The following year the International Olympic Committee took the initiative to convene the World Conference on Doping, which resolved to create a worldwide anti-doping agency.

In 1999, a joint foundation made up of world governments and international sports organizations established the World Anti-Doping Agency (WADA). The role of Finland in the creation of WADA was important because of Finland's first Presidency of the EU in 1999 and the special meeting of EU sports ministers that took place here. Partly due to this, Harri Syväsalmi, the Director of Sports at the Finnish Ministry of Education, was appointed as the first Secretary General of the new world agency. The first chairman of WADA was Richard Pound, a prominent IOC member from Canada and one of the main architects and promoters of the new agency. This Finnish-Canadian duo did much valuable work in getting WADA started and making it the credible force for clean sports that it is today. I was particularly proud to have worked with WADA at that time as a consultant.

Any form of cheating or dishonesty is perceived very negatively in Finland. As we have seen, Finland is one of the world's least corrupt countries and the trust index is among the highest in the world. There is often some significant stigma surrounding those who do not respect the rules to the letter. In this sense, Finns are perhaps a bit more rigid than other cultures to the east and south on the European continent.

At the 2001 Cross-Country Skiing World Championships in Lahti, Finland, the early sporting results were very good for the Finns. It seemed that the Finnish team was going to perform well on their home ground. Unfortunately, it suddenly all turned very sour. Jari Isometsä took the silver just before his previous doping test was confirmed as positive. The Finnish men also took the gold in the relay just before the entire team was brought in for testing. The overjoyed home crowd celebrated the victories of their heroes. The results of the doping tests, however, were a national and social catastrophe. Six of the best skiers on the Finnish team tested positive for doping. This included the world and Olympic champion Mika Myllylä, the much admired Olympic veteran and world champion Harri Kirvesniemi and four other elite skiers. They all tested positive for an illegal cover-up substance called Hemohes, which helps bring back down the levels of hemoglobin after the probable use of hemoglobin enhancing EPO or blood doping. The story made the front pages of the main Finnish media for weeks on end. A pillar of Finnishness seemed to have crumbled, and an irremovable stain on the national pride had spoiled the ideal many Finns had of their beloved elite athletes.

In February 2001, Harri Syväsalmi was working at the Skiing World Championships in Lahti, Finland as the Secretary General of WADA. He recalls that the idea of conducting a surprise test of the entire Finnish team came from his suggestion to the leadership of the Finnish Ski Federation.[13] This straightforward request from the Finnish Ski Federation is consistent with a strong and nationally shared belief in Finnish honesty and fair play. This time, the feeling of abuse of trust was devastating. Emotions were running high. Syvässalmi even received a death threat. Luckily it turned out to be a just drunken insurance salesman who could not bear to see his country's reputation being dragged through the mud.

For many years after this, the national media was not as kind as it once was toward elite sports in Finland. The bad press affected to some degree the general support sponsors and governments were ready to provide. The national press agency STT had a particular bone to pick with the skiing federation because it had been taken to court by the federation a year before the Lahti scandal for "falsely" reporting on the federation's alleged doping program. The ramifications of that case, combined with the events of Lahti in 2001, are still being processed in the Finnish courts over ten years later. This is one sad Finnish story that has dragged on for over ten years, and that culminated with the dramatic death of Mika Myllylä in July of 2011.

This exceptional Finnish tale of organized dishonesty should serve as a warning about the darker side of *sisu* for Finns and for people from any country who may think of compromising longstanding moral values for short-term selfish gain. Some goals are just not worth bending or breaking the rules for. In addition to the quest for personal success, these Finnish skiers were apparently willing to do anything to make their country proud of them on the rare occasion of the world championships being held in Finland. They could not have failed more spectacularly in their mission. Misplaced *sisu* is a dangerous force that can make even the best of us, from anywhere in the world, do the wrong thing.

WADA guy

I have been very fortunate in Finland not to have been subjected to any form of foreigner-targeted violence. Despite my dark looks and my funny accent, I have been lucky not to be at the wrong place at the wrong time. Many Finns themselves have not been so lucky in the face of others indulging in the kind of drinking that triggers unfortunate violence from time to time.

There is one incident, however, when for a few seconds I believed I was going to face some random violence in a public place. I was attending a telecom event in downtown Helsinki. I unfortunately still had a winter coat from my consulting stint at WADA. The coat was warm and a great conversation piece. The word WADA did not mean much to anyone in the world or in Finland prior to the year 2001, other than in Japan where it is a common surname. However, it developed instant brand recognition in Finland after the Lahti doping scandal.

I entered a downtown Helsinki bar in my WADA coat the same week as the scandal broke. Two men were getting visibly drunk at the counter. Oddly, they wore cross-country ski clothes. They were indulging in a nice cocktail of humor and shame. They looked straight at me and started to shout the name that had been on the lips of every Finn that week: "WADA! WADA!!!"

The bar turned dead quiet and all eyes were fixed upon the foreign looking guy who was working for WADA. For a few seconds, the tension in the room made me feel that this might be my last living moment. Finns tend to be unpredictable in bars and intense emotions of broken national pride were reaching scary peaks. Faced with a difficult situation, I used my secret weapon in the face of the dark side of *sisu*: Canadian humor.

I promptly walked up to the inebriated skiers, pulled the top of the tight elastic ski pants out from their waist and looked straight at their privates. I them told them in an official tone and with my funny Finnish accent that they had passed the test and that they could carry on drinking as much as they liked. Suddenly, the ice in the air started to break with a roll of bar-wide laughter, and the day and my Canadian butt were saved.

CHAPTER 5
Being yourself

My parents shared not only an improbable love;
they shared an abiding faith in the possibilities of
this nation. They would give me an African name,
Barack, or blessed, believing that in a tolerant
America your name is no barrier to success.

Barack Obama

If anybody would have told you in 2007 that a man called
Barack Hussein Obama would become the next President of
the United States of America, I am sure you, like many Europeans and Americans, would have thought it unlikely. The
Barack Obama story is inspiring in many ways and brings out
what most Europeans and Finns find most admirable about
the USA: a special blend of modern open-mindedness and
avant-garde uniqueness.

From a European perspective the accession of Obama to
power reinforces the widely held belief that everything is possible on the "new continent." It will probably be some time
before we see the son or a daughter of an African immigrant
as the president of any European state. That day, however, is
certainly closer because of the Obama presidency.

What is perhaps most inspiring about this chapter's opening quote is that Barack Obama believed in his parents' vision of an egalitarian and non-discriminatory society. He could well have used his nickname "Barry" in an attempt to please a wider American audience, but he chose to be himself and to use his own unique name. He, like many other successful persons, came to the simple conclusion that it is only when you are being genuinely and powerfully yourself that you can realize your full potential.

Genuineness and self-confidence make people believe in you. Personal and even business success usually escapes you if you try to be something you are not. Paradoxically, by narrowing down your persona or personal brand to what it really is, you actually become more universal and meaningful to a vast majority of people who are also looking deep within themselves for their lost or dormant authenticity.

If you ask some of the world's leading adventurers or mountain climbers, they will tell you that it is the uniqueness of the goal that makes the journey worthwhile. They all have set out to do what has never or seldom been done before. For the veteran climber Peter Habeler from Austria, it was to be the first to climb Mount Everest without oxygen. For Dominick Arduin it was to be the first woman to ski alone to the geographic North Pole. For the Finnish team of Veikka Gustafsson and Patrick Degerman it was to climb a mountain that had never been climbed before. They found and ultimately climbed this "virgin mountain" deep in Antarctica and baptized it, quite appropriately, Mount Sisu.

These adventurers make it into the history books because of their uniqueness, their authentic daring and the confidence they have in achieving their goals. In our previous chapter on *sisu* we saw that the journey itself was at the heart of the transformation. That still holds true at this stage; however, the important addition at this level of the model is that the choice of the goal has a tremendous impact on the nature of the resulting transformation.

The more personal the objectives and unique the venture, the more profound and meaningful is the ensuing transformation. You must choose your own peaks to climb and directions to follow based on your own personal compass. Climbing the wrong mountain is like driving down the wrong road. It doesn't get you very far and doesn't give you all that you are really looking for. A lot of energy goes partly wasted, but at least much can be learned about charting a better and more personal course for the next time around.

An interesting story of finding your own personal peak or destination is the case of the young Ben Saunders from the UK who, at the age of 26, succeeded in 2006 where Dominick Arduin failed. After skiing 800 miles in 10 weeks, and enduring the deep freeze and facing the hungry polar bears, he arrived precisely at point 90.00 on the globe and said to himself: "Oh my God! There is nothing there." Somehow he expected something more. At that point he was already preparing his next adventure, where there would be something even more super-human for him to achieve.[1] There are a dozen persons who have walked on the moon. Over 2000 people have already climbed Mount Everest. However, only four courageous individuals have walked or skied to the North Pole and lived to tell their story.

Who remembers the name of the second man to walk on the moon, after Neil Armstrong? His name is Edwin Aldrin and he is interestingly absent from our collective memory. The point here is that the first to arrive at a specific point where no person has gone before almost always receives exponential visibility and rewards compared to those who follow. This may seem unfair but it clearly shows the importance of finding and exploiting pursuits that are truly unique and genuine. These singular endeavors are ultimately those that people commit to memory and have the greatest collective impact and ability to inspire.

FIGURE 5-1: **The Holy Grail of being yourself**

Figure 5-1 presents the three main drivers of being your-self. They are healthy self-**confidence**, convincing **authenticity** and unique **personality**. At this last stage of our climb up the Possibility Model we find the gem that finally unlocks infinite possibilities for those who have already come quite far up the winding climb of success. Note that the three first letters of the elements sitting on top of our model form an easy to remember acronym: C.A.P. The acronym is fitting here because the elements indeed form the cap or top of the Possibility Model. Those who have embraced and assimilated this C.A.P. are indeed on top of their world.

These three key elements are put together here in the form a grail. The grail can become a holy treasure if it is well understood and acted upon. Though it may seem like the most natural of all the levels covered so far, being yourself is indeed the hardest level on the road to success because there is no map and no manual. No one can tell you the solution or the right direction but yourself.

Another dimension of the Possibility Model is its progression inwards as much as upward. The higher up in the model you are, the deeper you actually go into yourself. Indeed the first levels of the Model deal more with elements which are external to yourself. Open-mindedness is about letting in more of the external world and its endless possibilities. Trial and error is also externally focused. It is an attempt to test theories externally such as the chemical reactions, technical processes, consumer behavior patterns, etc.

At the level of working harder and smarter, the model begins to shift its focus towards the internal workings of the mind and behavior. At this stage, successes-in-the-making correlate more with what individuals and groups can do about themselves. The application of discipline in effort and the more active use of your intelligence are mainly driven internally. At the level of *sisu* we go beyond externally focused trial and error and focus on introspection and making changes that allow us to make courageous leaps of faith and muster enough internal determination to complete that sometimes painful last mile towards success.

Finally, being yourself is the most internally driven quest on the road to success. It is about going deep into the fabric of your identity and using it as a natural lever in the battle for positive differentiation. It is the discovery and the development of our unique and authentic appeal to the outside world.

A nice Finnish image to communicate this aspect of the Possibility Model would be a large segment of a tree trunk. The oldest and strongest part of the tree, the heartwood, is its center and that is where being yourself belongs. It is the spine that holds everything together and upon which, with time, grow layers of faculties that allow the entire tree to become wider and taller. The four other levels of the Possibility Model are more remote from the solid core of

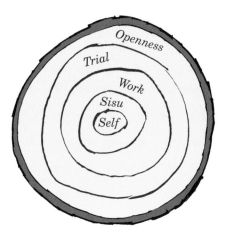

FIGURE 5-2: **The Possibility Model tree rings**

the identity but equally important in allowing uniqueness of self to grow and take its place in the human ecosystem.

One of the best catch phrases that depicts the importance of finding and ultimately being yourself in your quest for personal, business and societal success is the one by Oscar Wilde: "Be yourself. Everybody else is taken." Wilde was one of the great personalities of the London cultural scene as a popular Edwardian playwright. He believed that England put people in a mold that inhibited the cultivation of original personality. His phrase on being yourself explains, in my opinion, the simple yet fundamental correlation between the assertion of self and being successful. The enemy of innovation is imitation.

The enemy of success is trying to be someone that you are not. In this final chapter we will look at Finnish examples that exemplify the challenges and rewards of being yourself. These stories depict the surprising difficulty of finding that one very special and personal way to reach the ultimate frontier of our common quest for personal, business and societal success.

5.1 Getting personal

Knowing others is wisdom,
knowing yourself is enlightenment

Lao Tzu

Our personality is what distinguishes us from other human beings. It is our social fingerprint. The more our personal character features depart from the norm of a specific community, the more visibility and potentially the more interest we are able to generate. A strong personality can be a blessing or a curse depending on what you do with it. If it is combined with the courage to stand out and to use it constructively, then it can become a formidable asset in the generation of success. If, conversely, you are afraid to bring out your personality or do not find a venture where it can be optimally leveraged, then it is probably more of a burden than a blessing.

Corporations also have personalities. They are the special mission or *raison d'être* of each individual company. Corporate personality is made up of the unique set of products, services, experiences and brands a company has on offer. Company offerings and communication methods are potentially the inimitable smiles and expressions corporations display through their public face. Their unique catch phrases and slogans are the familiar voices that we instantly recognize from the noise of the crowd.

Countries have a personality as well. They are made up of the unique set of recurring personal features of their people, the special aspects of national geography, history and experience that make each country distinctive. The use of national brands, based on these differentiating attributes, has become a major new area of brand positioning for countries that wish to communicate their uniqueness to the world. Forging a national brand is about finding the natural common denominators of the national identity that can be credibly communicated globally as a positive differentiator among the planet's rich diversity of cultures and places.

To many who have had superficial contacts with Finns, the first impression of Finnish personality is usually not very strong. In many Western cultures the expression "having a personality" refers to things like flamboyance, extroverted charisma and a high degree of self-assurance. On the surface, most Finns would rate relatively low using these criteria. Some foreign observers are indeed left with the impression that Finns have a weak and even unimpressive personality. This is mostly due to language and cultural barriers.

As we have seen, most Finns value functional communication and even silence more than many people do in other cultures. Many in Finland believe that the "frills" that cultures often add to their communication takes away some of the credibility of the message. For this reason, the degree of extroverted communication in Finland is usually a few notches below what is common in other European and North American cultures. An insightful joke on this topic is one from Minister Alexander Stubb: What is the difference between introverts from Finland and introverts from other countries? Generally introverts look at your shoes when you talk to them. Finnish introverts, however, look at their own shoes when you are talking to them.

If we define personality simply as a the set of features that make a person unique, then Finnish personality can be qualified as relatively strong because you can instantly identify it. If some of the cultures of Northern Europe

seem close to each other from an outsider's perspective, the Finnish culture may actually be the one that is the most conspicuous. A Finn will usually stand out precisely because he or she does not stand out as much as the others do. This particular type of uniqueness can be useful or disastrous depending on the context.

The former Formula One world champion Kimi Räikkönen's communication style has often been criticized by some in Finland and elsewhere as being too "minimalistic." Nevertheless, he has had millions of fans from Melbourne to Montreal who just love the "ice man" from Finland precisely because he does not communicate the way everyone else does. He speaks like an animated block of ice, which enhances his nerves-of-steel image and which is actually very fitting for a world champion of Formula One racing. Branding yourself or your company can be like a bout of communicative judo. You can essentially transform a unique personal feature that is perceived as a weakness and change it into a surprising strength.

Normality vs. uniqueness

Throughout this book we have seen numerous examples of Finnish uniqueness. Finns are indeed unique when it comes to their combined levels of education, R&D, trust, invention, collective well-being, closeness to nature and mastery of the all-important *sisu*. These are all attributes that form a good part of the Finnish identity and its positive uniqueness. They are the elements that can form the basis for sustainable success if they are courageously displayed in the appropriate context.

As we have seen in earlier chapters, the enemy of innovation is imitation. At the stage of being yourself, you can similarly say that the enemy of uniqueness is normality.

The norm offers people everywhere a safe refuge for living their lives. It demands little and gives life a sense of predictability that many of us need. However, normality produces little in terms of personal actualization or corporate differentiation. Uniqueness is the ultimate driver of personal and corporate value. The paradox is that most of us are happy living a "normal" and predictable life. Normality is the undercurrent of society that allows unique personalities to make waves. From this perspective, Finnish culture sometimes looks, on its surface, like a lake as opposed to a wave-rich ocean. However, lakes offer features and possibilities that oceans do not, and vice versa.

Asserting a sense of powerful uniqueness is a constant challenge for many but it is now, more than ever, a critical driver of economic success. Companies can no longer afford to simply make incremental changes and improvements to their business processes. Challengers from all over the world, especially from the developing world, are increasingly able to produce similar goods and services more efficiently than their developed world predecessors. Quality engineering, for example, can now be found from many emerging countries with the rise of an exploding new population of skilled and less expensive labor. In India alone, there will soon be more engineers and consultants than there are inhabitants in the United States of America.

Another important driver of the demand for uniqueness is the magnitude of possibilities brought on by the creation of a new and immense virtual market place facilitated by the Internet. This digitalization of our world allows many more market players to leverage their uniqueness. The long tail theory of Chris Andersson is one way to understand this phenomenon.[2] Where the economics of the purely physical world allowed only a few hits made for mass consumption, the Internet has allowed an infinite number of unique niches to be able to prosper. It has even allowed niche players to receive surprising over-night success by spreading their uniqueness over the Internet at shocking speeds. Indeed, one of the barriers to the exploitation of uniqueness, the limited capacity of the physical world for delivering goods, services and information, has now been exponentially enhanced by the opening of the digital frontier. This transformation is also the central theme of Joseph Pine's recent book, appropriately called *Infinite Possibility*.[3]

These trends allow us to conclude that success in the future will be about personality and uniqueness. It is therefore critical for individuals, companies and nations to promote personality and harvest uniqueness, encouraging all of us to develop offerings that are powerfully unique. As we have seen throughout our journey up the possibility model, this is not easy. The road towards uniqueness and being yourself is singularly demanding. Most people are afraid to trade a life devoted to the norm for the risk of a life devoted to being unique.

This, I believe, is particularly true in Finland. For Finns, the cultural challenges of fostering uniqueness are visible at many stages of our model. The high level of education in Finland has had the potential downside of creating a culture that too often strives towards finding only one right answer and a "normal" way of doing things. The fear of making errors at the personal level, the lower confidence in intuition and the aversion to risk in business result in lower levels of entrepreneurship which, in turn, inhibits the commercialization of Finnish uniqueness.

Positive uniqueness

Uniqueness is a two-sided sword when it comes to achieving success. It cuts both ways in that it can cut you off from success if your uniqueness is positioned in a non-optimal way. Leveraging uniqueness in the quest of achieving success comes down to the positioning of a specific set of personal or corporate features in a particular context.

In figure 5-3, positive uniqueness is located at the top of the junction of two important success drivers: desirability and differentiation. These two important drivers begin with the letter D, hence the name of the model. Desirability expresses the level of demand for any given feature of individual or corporate personality. Differentiation refers to the relative distinctiveness of these same features. When these two drivers are laid down in the form of intersecting axes, they produce a simple yet compelling picture of personality feature-positioning.

The most attractive area in this graph is naturally located on the positive sides of both desirability and differentiation. Within this area four related areas emerge. They are characterized by the relative levels of desirability and differentiation achieved. At lower levels of both D's, the result can be described as being better than average.

If you enhance your desirability but remain low in differentiation, the result is a more competitive offering in a cluttered market. If differentiation is enhanced but desirability remains low, the result can be said to be personal but relatively less appealing. All of these positions fall short of

FIGURE 5-3:

The 2D model of positive uniqueness

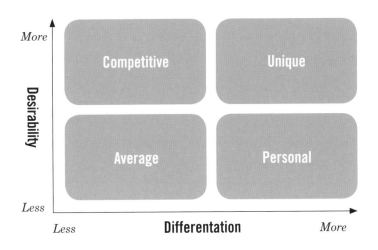

the optimal positioning of both enhanced desirability and differentiation. This is the place where you are positively unique and in a position to optimally leverage all that you are to significantly enhance your chances of achieving success.

At the personal level a good Finnish example of this is the career path of the Finnish ice dancing couple of Susanna Rahkamo and Petri Kokko.[4] These two great athletes began their career with an unimpressive last place at the European Championships in 1985. They would ultimately capture the gold medal at this event ten years later.

The relevance of their successful journey to the top of their art is marked by a very important lesson on the applicability of the 2D model of positive uniqueness. In addition to working harder and smarter, they understood that in this young sports discipline, artistic uniqueness was as important as the mastery of technical prowess. They recall an attempt to change coaches and a move from Germany to the United Kingdom, which gradually took away much of the uniqueness of their performing potential. In an attempt to become more competitive, they were becoming less unique.

Susanna Rahkamo remembers that this change of strategy was making her physically ill, to the point that they decided to move back to Germany and their original style of skating. The return to their zone of positive uniqueness paid off with a career that put them on top of the ice dancing world. The valuable insight they received is that it is futile to try to win by being anything other than yourself. It you don't win by being yourself you probably never will.

Another successful Finn is Sauli Niinistö who at the time of writing had officially declared his intention to run for the Presidency of Finland. Niinistö has a long and distinguished career as a politician, often receiving record-breaking results at the polls. When asked what he believes made this possible, he referred to an observation of one of his aides who said that he portrayed a special image of "Pedant-Bohemian" that many electors could believe in and ultimately relate to.[5] He combined his stern professionalism (pedant) with a special kind of non-conformity (bohemian) that made him positively unique in the eyes of the electorate.

The exercise of assembling unique personal and corporate features and positioning them in a positive manner around the axis of desirability and differentiation is indeed a constant in all of the personal and corporate success stories covered in this book. This kind of personality positioning is one key to success. The next section offers a few more compelling Finnish examples that drive this point home.

What Finnish personality?

After all we have seen through our voyage up the Possibility Model, punctuated with stories of Finnish success and some stories of failures, the adjectives that would best define the Finnish personality would include: reserved, silent, knowledgeable, fair, risk-averse, trustworthy, natural, humble, hardworking, brave and direct. Some would use qualifiers close to these that are maybe a few degrees more positive or negative, but by and large this is where much of Finnish uniqueness lies. These attributes constitute the raw material that can continue to allow many Finns to position themselves for success.

Of course these are to a certain degree stereotypes that should not work to exclude or inhibit Finns who don't fit this bill and who want to develop themselves on an entirely different slate of uniqueness. In a recent Gallup poll, some of the traditional values identified here are changing in certain segments of the population. This can only be good for the differentiation that Finland and many other countries will need from their citizens in the years to come.[6]

The fairly recent country brand report used many of these features to come up with an elaborate account of how Finland, as a country, should position itself. Based on many of the personality features identified above, and the geographical and historical profile of the country, the brand commission came up with a challenging "Mission for Finland." This mission focuses not only on current national strengths but also creates a collective challenge for what is possible in the future.

One of the most interesting positionings proposed by the report is the one that presents Finland as a world-class problem solving nation. In a very self-confident opening line, Finland's Country Brand Delegation raises the reader's expectations: "How Finland will demonstrate its strengths by solving the world's most wicked problems."[7] The report eloquently positions Finland as a world leader in education, functionality, and nature-friendliness. This mission and national positioning convince because they are wisely based on genuine Finnish uniqueness.

In Chapter 1 we explained how Finland is a world leader of the "open mind" with its topflight education and egalitarian culture. In Chapter 3 we saw that Finland is indeed very "functional" because it works harder and smarter in a culture that enhances cutting-edge efficiencies. One of the fresh features to come out of this report is its atypical level of self-assertiveness, putting Finland on a course that will require taking risks and developing a new level of innovative enterprise. This was a Finnish challenge and a source of concern that we identified in Chapter 2 dealing with trial and error. The following stories of leveraging traditional and avant-garde Finnish uniqueness should make us believe that this can indeed be done.

A Nobel personality: President Martti Ahtisaari

Martti Ahtisaari is one of the world's most accomplished diplomats and statesmen. He is the Nobel Peace Prize winner of 2008 and served as Finland's 10th President. He began his career as a teacher in the City of Oulu in northwest Finland. His first international assignment was in Pakistan, where he did development work as a young teacher trainer in 1960. This led him to join Finland's foreign office and later become an ambassador of his country to several nations in southern Africa.

Between 1973 and 1976 Martti Ahtisaari was Finland's Ambassador in Tanzania. He held several UN roles in Namibia from 1975–1990, and as UN Special Representatives he oversaw the country's transition to independence from April 1989 to March 1990. Subsequently, both he and his wife were made honorary Namibian citizens.

In 1994, despite having a relatively unknown persona in terms of national politics, Ahtisaari was elected President of the Republic of Finland. During his term of office, Finland joined the EU and assumed its presidency in 1999; Helsinki hosted the Clinton-Yeltsin summit that set the foundation for the expansion of NATO to some parts of Eastern Europe; his administration worked closely with the governments of Russia and the USA to negotiate an end to the hostilities in Kosovo with the notorious Slobodan Milosevic.

After his retirement from office in 2000, he established his own organization for the furtherance of global conflict resolution: the Crisis Management Initiative (CMI). The most notable achievement of this period of his career is the peace agreement that he brokered between the Free Aceh Movement and the government of Indonesia in 2005. Finally in 2008, Ahtisaari received the Nobel Peace Prize for his achievements over his 30 year career as an international peace broker.

One of the interesting aspects of the Ahtisaari story is that it begins during the difficult years of the Winter and Continuation Wars with the Soviet Union. Born in the Finnish Karelian City of Viipuri in 1937, he and his family were among the 400 000 Karelian refugees, a tenth of the Finnish population at the time, who needed to leave their homes and move to other areas in Finland.

This is a difficult start in life for anyone, but it served as a very formative experience for someone who would one day have to deal with the complex issues of negotiating peace and, among other subjects, the fate of war refugees on a global scale. It is commendable that Ahtisaari was able to turn this difficult part of his and his nation's past into a personal and professional strength. In many ways, Ahtisaari is a personal symbol of Finland's spectacular mid-20th Century turnaround.

When I asked him what Finnish attribute is the most conducive to generating personal and professional success, President Ahtisaari told me he believes that it is Finnish honesty and trustworthiness.[8] He also believes that this important feature of Finnish culture was a critical factor in his professional success as a broker of international peace settlements. Ahtisaari's special blend of humility and straightforwardness made him a man that many people from very different cultures could easily trust.

Interestingly, Ahtisaari stresses that the trust level he was able to achieve in these challenging settings was not an exercise of impartiality. As opposed to a judge in a court of law, a peace negotiator is valued more for his honesty than his impartiality. He made it a point to communicate clearly with all parties where he stood on every issue. This honest display of his personal views gave him credibility with both sides of the negotiation.

In many ways Martti Ahtisaari's successes find their roots in his unique personality and to some extent in many of the positive values found in Finnish culture. If you analyze his career through the stages of the Possibility Model you find that he indeed built himself a solid base for generating his success as a peace broker. His formative years as a teacher in Finland gave him a very good base for the open-mindedness he would need later in life.

He received a good education and ultimately became fluent in three languages. He is still adamant today on the importance of speaking Swedish in Finland. This is an important feature of the national identity and a key to opening your mind to another culture than your own. In this regard his three determining years in Pakistan as a teacher-of-teachers opened his mind very early and exposed him to the tolerance needed to function in a truly multicultural environment.

Ahtisaari clearly knew how to handle long processes of trial and error. He took the risk of bringing his family out to live in many challenging areas of the world. He also experienced long periods of negotiations with warring factions that seemed unwilling to compromise. In fact, his first mission in Namibia took a good twelve years to bring to a successful conclusion. In this way, you can say that he displayed some good old-fashioned Finnish *sisu* in the face of long and frustrating years of deadlock in negotiations.

Ahtisaari even faced the threat of violence from those with an interest in his negotiations failing. He was not afraid to look at his negotiators and tell them straight in the eyes that they were not serious about peace. This directness made him even more effective in his role. In the end, Ahtisaari, with his unique set of personal and professional strengths, was able to make the lives of millions around the world more peaceful than they were before. Ahtisaari may well be remembered as one of the great Finnish ambassadors of *sisu*, who reminded the world when accepting the Nobel Peace Prize that "Peace is a question of will."

Birds with a global personality:
Rovio's Angry Birds

Finland has been a hotbed for global innovation in the area of digital gaming. Sulake Corporation's Habbo Hotel came out in 2000 and revolutionized the world of gaming. The game was one of the first to allow players to interact socially through the creation of avatars, and to personalize their own digital environments. The success of Max Payne, the box office hit among console video games from the Finnish gaming studio Remedy Entertainment, is also one of the notable Finnish victories in the global digital gaming scene of the past ten years.

More recently, Finland has served as the launch pad for one the most successful mobile games in history. Rovio, a Finnish gaming development company, has taken the world of gaming by storm with its Angry Birds. It is a puzzle video game that involves a perpetual battle between wingless angry birds and ugly green pigs that have stolen the birds' eggs. In the game, the player uses an old-fashioned slingshot to launch the birds at the pigs positioned around or within a variety of structures, with the purpose of destroying all of the pigs on the playing field.

At the time of writing, the game had been installed more than 300 million times. The game is growing at a dizzying pace of 1 million downloads per day. It has an active fan-base of 40 million players every month who play the game a total of 200 million hours a day. Based on Google Trends' Search Monitor Index, it has surpassed the immense popularity of Facebook's Farmville and the popular digital game Bejeweled. All of this has happened in less than two years and has consumed the attention of adults and children alike all over the world. Based on this impressive data you can say that

Rovio's Angry Birds is the most recent Finnish Miracle in the field of international business.

Rovio began in 2003 with a team of three young students from the Helsinki University of Technology: Niklas Hed, Jarno Väkeväinen and Kim Dikert. They were encouraged to form the company by the current Chief Marketing officer, Peter Vesterbacka, who was working for Hewlett-Packard at the time. Until 2009 the company was doing mostly games for other gaming companies. They made the game King of the Cabbage World and got a distribution deal through Digital Chocolate, another Finnish gaming company. They also did some work-for-hire with games like Need for Speed Carbon for Electronic Arts.

In 2009, the company's new CEO, Mikael Hed, began to shift Rovio's focus toward making games that the company could own itself. Rovio identified the iPhone and its touchscreen technology as a major new opportunity for mobile gaming. According to Vesterbacka, the company's 12 employees at that time set out to build the best mobile game ever. He says the company used typical Finnish analytical skills and combined them with important insights on where the industry was going.[9]

Senior game designer Jaakko Iisalo is credited for drawing the first Angry Birds characters in 2009. With all this momentum, the company received financing from the well-known Accel Partners VC firm to the tune of 42 million USD, which according to analysts gives the company a valuation of nearly 300 million Euros. Vesterbacka is bolder in his assessment of the company's valuation. He notes that Zynga, the gaming company behind Farmville and CityVille, is facing an IPO with an estimated value of 15 to 20 billion dollars. Rovio's Angry Birds has clearly surpassed the popularity of Farmville and Cityville, so Vesterbacka feels that Rovio should be worth at least as much as Zynga is.

Rovio's Angry Birds have accumulated many high-profile fans for its addictive, clever and endlessly challenging game. The Prime Minister of the United Kingdom is said to enjoy the iPad version of the game. Even the prominent author Salman Rushdie has claimed to be a master player. For many, Steve Jobs' iPad is simply a machine that allows people to play Angry Birds. At the Global Economic Summit in St. Petersburg, President Medvedev spoke out to state that many of the Russian bureaucrats take some time to play Angry Birds every day and that he thinks this is not a bad thing.

Angry Birds is a splendid case example of a Finnish miracle that has travelled up the stages of the Possibility Model at record speed. Vesterbacka states that the most significant success story in Finnish history has been the creation of an education system and a society that have produced an impressive amount of professional capability. He is convinced that the success of Rovio and the Angry Birds is the result of this Finnish "open mind." The absence of useless hierarchies and a culture that promotes knowledge, freedom and meritocracy makes Vesterbacka say that, in effect, the true "American Dream" is really the one made in Finland.

The Rovio story is also one of significant trial and error. Angry Birds is the company's 52nd game. It is the result of both a new insightful business strategy and the highly analytical process of cognitive trial and error that produced a game which would be irresistible for tens of millions of players down to the small yet perfect detail of a laughing green pig after your failed attempts.

The work utility function at Rovio is world-class. With an original team of only 12 people in 2009, they took on and defeated companies in their segment with thousands of employees such as EA and Disney. The level of intelligence and efficient working culture is clearly the best example of modern Finnish functionalism at work. The company has demonstrated a great deal of cool-headed *sisu* in believing that it could challenge the giants of the industry and win. In particular, it was adamant in not selling out to any of the larger players on its road to the top. Ultimately, Rovio found a game that brought together all of its unique experience and talent.

Vesterbacka states that this Finnish team has overcome one of the challenging features of the Finnish psyche, which has been an unnecessary amount of humility. Breaking this sometimes self-defeating national habit, Vesterbacka goes out of his way to strongly communicate the company's individuality and uniqueness when he shows up at all of the company's public events worldwide wearing Angry Birds t-shirts or sweatshirts when everyone else is in a suit and tie.

Rovio is not cocky but, with the Rovio leaders' great vision of becoming a multi-billion dollar entertainment company along the lines of Marvel, they are determined to be number one in every business segment they enter. This new kind of Finnish self-confidence is in some ways reminiscent of the Nokia of the 1990's, where the sky seemed to be the limit.

5.2 Authenticity

Getting real

At the center of the concept of being yourself, and as a prerequisite for finding and leveraging your uniqueness, is the need for authenticity. Being powerfully unique is often not enough to achieve your desired level of personal and business success. For your uniqueness to have value it must be perceived as authentic and genuine. This is necessarily a question of communication, because authenticity is something that is rendered in the eyes of others while uniqueness is usually something that involves a mostly solitary exploration into who we are.

In many cases, authenticity is the acid test for your own perceived uniqueness. Lack of perceived authenticity may come from an incorrect assessment of who you really are. Finding one's true self is not a simple straightforward process. It is, however, a necessary step to achieving authenticity. If your identity as a person, a company or even as a country is not clear to you, it most likely will not be clear to others. People in general are attracted by the real and easily reject the fake. This is why once you have found and developed your uniqueness, you must start getting real.

The process of getting real is about being systematic in being what you say you are. People get the impression that your uniqueness is real when your words and your behavior are aligned. It is indeed the alignment of uniqueness with authenticity that creates the most possibilities for all of us.

In the realm of philosophy it is interesting to point to Jean-Jacques Rousseau's "Le Bon Sauvage" and the existentialists like Jean-Paul Sartre, who praised the self untainted by the outside world as the pinnacle of authenticity. In the arts, the concept is mostly related to the unique value attached to the source and origin of a piece or work. In almost all of the social sciences, as in our personal lives, the genuine is always celebrated and the phony is looked down upon.

The rise of authenticity as an important part of doing business has risen dramatically over the past decade. The rendering of authenticity by creating genuine customer experiences, and by building brands that communicate the genuine value of a company's offerings, has been one of the rising concerns of marketing executives worldwide.[10] The rapid growth of companies like Facebook and Twitter are partly based on the authenticity of their image and offerings. The generalized belief in the uniqueness of these companies, their perceived authenticity among their customers, is at the core of their corporate value.

Branding and market positioning are crucial to the efforts to highlight the authenticity of a company's unique offering. For example, many Finnish products position themselves as being of high quality and high functionality. This is the case with Marimekko's textiles and accessories. They have a special authentic story attached to them. They cost more, they are unique and they are more durable than other such products on the market. They are also positioned distinctively and separately from premium luxury products such as Louis Vuitton or Hermes.

By changing the marketing positioning of a Marimekko bag by either distributing it through a low-cost retailer such as K-mart or conversely by putting on price tags in the luxury product range, you remove an important part of this product-perceived authenticity. A bag bought at K-mart cannot be expected to last. Conversely, a luxury price tag weakens the claim of functionality as a primary driver for the brand. Thus a unique product can be rendered inauthentic by positioning it in an improper manner.

In the field of promotion it is clear that a company's brand and its corporate communications are among the most powerful tools in the rendering of its authenticity. A strong brand communicates corporate identity and, more importantly, it makes a recurring promise on behalf of the corporation to its current and prospective customers. In many cases a brand is an important driver of corporate authenticity because it blends the special cluster of ideas that have generated the unique set of products and services of a company into a compelling and believable message.

It is interesting to note that in some cases acknowledging some aspects of fakeness in a company's offering can paradoxically enhance its authenticity. Joseph Pine and James

Gilmore give a series of example of this in their book on authenticity.[12] Disneyland is perhaps the clearest example they give of something that is known to be fake but is perceived as providing very real experiences. To recognize and leverage this type of dichotomy is one of the key success factors of the art of rendering authenticity.

The same can be said of birds without wings and the green pigs of the Angry Birds game. They are clearly fake but provide a very unique and real experience. The leveraging of this tension between fake and real provides additional possibilities in creating the desired level of perceived authenticity in the marketplace.

Finnish authenticity

At the personal level, Finns come across as very genuine. It is often their no-frills style of communication and an almost genetically endowed humility that makes most Finns come across as authentic. Of course, the context and purpose of the communication is important. Most North American agents for performers would consider these personal features inappropriate for an aspiring stand-up comedian. However, in most social contexts Finnish people are perceived as trustworthy because of their unique form of authenticity.

Finns do fairly well in communicating, in their own special way, that they are for real. This is because Finnish culture is one that promotes saying things as they are: being clear about who you are and doing what you say you are going to do. This is a simple yet effective formula that explains the great value attributed to genuineness in Finland, and that illustrates why many cultures find Finns easy to believe.

I once referred a Finnish arbitration case to one of my lawyer friends in Montreal. He came back to me after taking many depositions from Finnish witnesses for his case in Finland and said to me: "You know. Throughout my entire career, I think I have never heard such a series of highly believable witnesses as I have heard in Finland." Finns are indeed a believable bunch of people. It is in part because of this that they have achieved, in many disciplines, very good social and economic results. In this section we look at some very authentic Finnish stories to illustrate this point.

An authentic Finn: Saku Koivu

Saku Koivu is a professional ice hockey player who comes from one of the most authentic ice hockey families in Finland. His father was the long-standing coach of TPS, the renowned ice-hockey club of their native Turku, Finland's former capital and its fourth largest city. His younger brother Mikko Koivu is also a successful ice hockey player. The Koivus represent a special brand of people within their sport. All three men are associated with an excellent work ethic, world-class competence and a gentlemen-like demeanor that exudes fair play.

In 1995, Saku Koivu was one of the young players of the Finnish National team who won the world championships against the country's archrival in sports: Sweden. His younger brother Mikko repeated this feat sixteen years later, this time as captain of the team. Their father, Jukka, was one of the TV commentators during the last World Championships. In the eyes of most Finns, this family eats and breathes ice hockey with an uncontestable display of genuine love for the game.

In 1995, Saku Koivu began to play for the legendary Montreal Canadiens. I remember meeting up with him in 1998 at a press conference in Turku where we were promoting our Winter Olympic bid just before his departure for another season in Montreal. I congratulated him on his great work for my beloved Montreal Canadiens, but I mostly was impressed by how he had already made his mark on the culture of the City of Montreal, which is a predominantly French-speaking city with a very rich ice-hockey heritage.

Koivu ultimately served as the captain of the Canadiens' for nine of his thirteen seasons with the club. This makes him, along with the celebrated Jean Béliveau, the longest serving captain in the team's history. Koivu was the first European to be named captain of the Montreal Canadiens. In 2008, the NHL's *Impact! Magazine* ranked him among the top ten team captains of all time, along with the likes of Mark Messier and Mario Lemieux.

Koivu's long career at the Montreal Canadiens was an eventful one. It began brilliantly. In his first year, Koivu ranked fourth in scoring amongst NHL rookies. The following season, Koivu was among the NHL's leading scorers before suffering a knee injury. This would be one in a series of many physical injuries Koivu would have to endure. The most impressive aspect of Koivu's carreer was his resilience and perhaps his *sisu*. Despite the multiple injuries he incurred, Koivu always managed to push on through and make a very decent number of season points for his team.

His biggest health challenge came in 2001 when he was diagnosed with cancer. He sat out the entire 2001–2002 season but made a remarkable comeback the next year to a crowd that gave him a standing ovation. For his courage and off-the-ice team leadership while undergoing cancer treatment, he was awarded the Bill Masterton Memorial Trophy following the 2002 playoffs.

He made an amazing recovery and in 2002–2003 scored his way to a personal best of 71 points. He would actually do even better in 2006 with a total of 75 points. The following year he would meet some more health challenges with a game accident that gravely impaired the sight in one of his eyes. Despite this and all of his trials, Saku Koivu has accumulated over 700 points in his 15 years in the NHL.

Koivu left the Montreal Canadiens in 2009 to join the Anaheim Mighty Ducks. In January 2011, he returned to Montreal for the first time to play against his old team. The crowd gave him a standing ovation. In addition to his obvious demonstration of Finnish *sisu* over the years, I believe that other aspects of his Finnishness have won him the hearts of most Quebecers.

First, at 1.78 meters and 81 kilos, Koivu is on the smaller side of the typical dimensions for NHL players, which has made some scenes in front of the opponent's net look like a bout between David and Goliath. The other important factor was his love and loyalty toward the game and to his team. Everyone was impressed with this talented millionaire from Finland who would simply never give up. His communication style, both in English and in his elementary French, exuded total genuineness. This won him the admiration of his teammates and the affection of much of the French Canadian population.

SAKU
in the hearts of
Les Boys

A scene in the popular French Canadian movie *Les Boys* demonstrates the place Saku Koivu has won in the hearts of his adoptive culture. The movie is about a bunch of guys playing in a Montreal garage league who get involved in a hockey game to save the pub that belongs to the team's sponsor.

They are a fairly washed up and out-of-shape bunch of ice hockey amateurs who, in truly Rocky-like style, end up winning the big game to the disbelief of their large and well-trained opponents. From a Finnish perspective, the telling part comes at the end of the movie.

The star player is celebrating the team victory with his wife in Stan's pub with the other players. She has just told him, during the game, that she is pregnant. Speaking in a tone of deep love for his wife and for the game of hockey, he says to her while touching her stomach: "If it is a boy I would want to call him Saku." She replies: "Saku Painchaud? Doesn't that sound weird to you?" Her reaction visibly upsets him.

Comic effect aside, this short scene communicates volumes about the place Saku Koivu holds in the hearts of many Quebecers. He was perceived as authentic just by being powerfully himself. He used his personal uniqueness as a differentiating strength. He was inspiring both on and off the ice. Koivu was perceived as authentic because of his natural Finnish humility and his honest and fair work on the ice.

Trusting the natives

I have always found it interesting to see how some Finnish companies have leveraged their Finnish identity to position their offerings. The reference to this type of authenticity has produced positive results. The design company Marimekko is, again, a good example of a Finnish mix of original design, closeness to nature and high quality. This positioning has made the company a leader in Finland and has had positive results in selected international markets.

Finlandia Vodka is among the world's top premium vodka brands, and this branding is based on the authenticity of its place of origin and the look and feel of the coolest vodka in the world. Kalevala Koru, the Finnish jewelry manufacturer, is a splendid case of original authenticity based on the theme of Finland's national epic story of the Kalevala. In this market, the experience is largely about owning and wearing a part of Finnish history, an experience reinforced by the smart illusion that one is wearing jewels coming straight out of an archeological dig. The company, which is owned by the Kalevela Women's Federation, also has a foundation that supports the promotion of Finnish culture. This further enhances the genuineness of the company's mission.

Another successful company that has leveraged its Finnishness in its corporate communications is Nokia Tyres. This company broke off from the Nokia Corporation in 1988. It is the part of the Nokia group that was created at the turn of the last century and produced all types of rubber products, including the legendary Nokia rubber boots. The company has since then focused on manufacturing tires for cars and larger industrial vehicles. Its turnover exceeds 1 billion Euros, and it operates mostly in the Nordic Countries and Russia.

The company's uniqueness resides in its knowledge of what makes a great tire in general and winter tires in particular. This distinctiveness is based on extensive R&D, a long experience in producing tires and in dealing with extreme weather and road conditions that allow for rigorous winter-tire testing. The company is made up of "winter natives" with the experience and knowledge that make them unique. For many experts in the field, Nokia Tyres are the best winter tires in the world. They are a quality leader, not a cost leader.

One of the ways they render their authenticity is in their advertising. They want to communicate that they are the real gatekeepers of the secret of the most reliable winter tire on the market. Their claims in certain early advertisements went a little too far when they stated that they are the "only" company that understands winter tires. Though they may genuinely feel that this is the case, rules of advertising do not allow you to make exclusive claims of this sort. They then came up with a great corporate slogan: "Trust the natives." The message positions them as the natives of challenging terrain, including icy winter roads. It is a call to trust based on this claim of authenticity.

The advertising series that the company produced around the "Trust the Natives" concept is an intelligent use of exceptional authenticity and Finnishness in advertising. In most of the company's marketing campaigns over the past few years, we see Finns doing something genuine and extreme as a symbol of their native knowledge of rugged conditions. One campaign features a bear that ultimately turns out to be person, most likely a Finnish native of the wild who takes his bear suit off and starts to confidently drive off on a craggy country road. Another famous clip is one of a British hunter stumbling on a bunch of crazy Finns playing swamp football with their cars nearby.

I personally feel close to the Nokia Tyres brand because one of their Trust the Natives campaigns featured me as the main character of the advertisement. I played the role of an intense French explorer lost in the Arctic looking for real natives. In a slightly humoristic Jacques Cousteau style, I make the audience believe that we are seeking new life in the distant north. The French expedition finally finds a flagged pole planted in an ice-hole. The expedition believes that it is a place where the mysterious natives put their fishing nets under the ice. In the end, all that these French tourists find are two Finnish Arctic golfers in T-shirts asking the overdressed French explorers to get out of the way of their next play. This ad won a prize, probably because of its humorous rendition of Finnish authenticity, with its claim of winter nativity and winter tire technology leadership.

Finnish Tango

One of the most interesting cultural phenomena in Finland is Finnish Tango. It is unique in its blend of cultural influences and its surprising staying power among a large part of the Finnish population. The original tango comes, as we all know, from Argentina and is famous for its intensity, its dramatic moves and its sensuality. This art form, born in the Argentinean working class, came to Europe via travelling musicians in the early 20th century. By the 1930's, Finns were actively writing their own tangos, and after the wars, the genre spread quickly, developing mass appeal throughout the Finnish countryside.[12]

A large percentage of members of the post-war generation of Finland met their first mates on one of the thousands of tango dancing floors that swelled up during those years. The genre declined in relative popularity with the rise of rock n' roll but came into renewed popularity in 1985 with the launch of the now famous Tango Festival. This is a summer media extravaganza of sorts, televised to audiences sometimes reaching the levels for top-drawer political debates. Over 100 000 people have regularly attended the festival in Seinäjoki, a small town of 30 000 people in Western Finland. The event transforms the city streets into the largest tango dance floor in the world. The main tango festivals in Argentina today collect no more than 10 000 participants.

The secret of the success of the Finnish Tango is a paradox of authenticity. As we have mentioned earlier, the blend of fake and real elements can often create a creative and compelling offering. In this case, the Finnish Tango is totally perceived as a 100 percent genuine Finnish phenomenon even though it is built upon a foreign Argentinean base. The strength of the Finnish tango is its role as a platform for exorcising the Finnish soul. The foreign musical element is needed, as most of the famous lyrics speak of fantasy travels to lands unknown. This is the case, for instance, with the most famous Finnish tango: Satumaa (Land of Dreams).

In all other respects, Finnish tango captures many of the difficult themes Finns wrestle with in their everyday lives: solitude, lost love, inhibition and the like. All this is served on a plate of relative melancholy in minor keys. Much like the blues, which is also very popular in Finland, the Finnish Tango has offered Finns a cathartic cocktail of emotions they can easily relate to. In addition, the Tango has given Finns an opportunity to experience physical closeness in a culture that otherwise likes to keep a good distance between people and frowns upon things like hugging or kissing of acquaintances.

In 1993, the weekly CBS news program *60 Minutes* did an interesting piece on Finnish culture and the Finnish Tango.

The report falls into relative sensationalism when it depicts Finns as a unique breed of humans who are stone faced, sad, anti-social and silent. Of course, some of this is true to a degree. Fortunately, the piece is treated with good humor and includes one of the most charming and smiling singers of the genre, Arja Koriseva.

The story of one of Finland's most successful music business entrepreneurs is worth mentioning at this stage. Seppo Kulmala is a cheerful accordionist who, after playing with most of the great names of Finnish Tango from the 1960's, such as Olavi Virta and Laila Kinnunen, began to start up several ventures in the music business. Kulmala is the ultimate self-made man from relatively humble beginnings. As a boy, he saved money from running errands for the local flower shop in order to be able to buy the accordion he admired in a shop window.

After a successful career as a musician in popular dance halls, he decided to open a music shop of his own. This was followed by a music school and finally a management agency for the country's top dance hall performers. His company, Auraviihde, is the founder of the Finnish Tango Festival and is still the owner of the franchise for the event. In 2009, the turnover of the company was close to 14 million Euros. Auraviihde was sold by his two sons to Sony BMG in 2010. This is a tale of leveraged authenticity that produced a cultural institution as well as a profitable business.

When I first came to Finland my musician friends immediately introduced me to the Finnish Tango. I found it strange at the start, but then I slowly became attuned to its cathartic melancholy and its generally strong musicianship. I started thinking about participating in the Tango finals. Unfortunately my distinct foreign accent excluded me from the very pure and authentic Finnish that is spoken and sung at this event. But in another tale of making the impossible

possible, I finally made it to the Tango finals in my own genuine way.

It was a few nights before Christmas and crazy ideas were stirring in the Chaker household. For many years in a row, we have had the family of my friend Jukka Karjalainen over for some good food and Christmas cheer before the holidays. This usually includes having fun with the guitar and the piano. Jukka Karjalainen, who writes and performs under the name J. Karjalainen, is one of Finland's most prolific popular music composers of the past 30 years. He is also one of the recognized grand masters of the use of the Finnish language. Interestingly, when interviewed for this book, Karjalainen said he believed that the Finnish language is perhaps the most significant Finnish success story.[13]

On this particular evening I told Jukka of an idea that had been brewing in my mind. One of the great Finnish standards, or *iskelmä*, of recent times is a song called "André," sung by one of the most famous Tango queens in Finland, Marita Taavitsainen. It tells the tale of a Finnish girl who gets bored of Finland and leaves for the exotic vineyards of France. There she finds André and falls in love. In every Finnish standard, there must be a good dose of drama to make it work. This Finnish girl ultimately leaves her beloved André, promising that he will hear from her one day.

The idea that sprung to my mind was to write a sequel to this song, as would be common in French or American music culture. In Finland's relatively solitary music culture, this kind of thematic cross-referencing was unheard of. In our sequel, André would sing his side of the story to his beloved Marita. Jukka's face glistened with an emerging idea and then two days later he sent me a message saying "André. Marita is ready and it is great." From there the project got slightly out of hand and I ended up on national

TV with Marita and on the Iskelmä music charts for most of that summer.

The highlight of this experience was performing with Marita at the finals of the Tango festival. Personally, one of my best moments as an adoptive Finn was performing at the Tango festival finals. Culturally, though, the Tango festival is one of the most hermetically sealed events in the country. No foreigner really finds his or her way there as it is naturally and genuinely for Finns only. In many ways the festival is perceived as an authentic expression of *supisuomalaisuus* or extreme Finnishness.

First Marita went on stage and sang a few verses of her legendary André. Then I came on-stage speaking an introduction in French. I could almost feel part of the audience saying to themselves: "What the hell is he doing there? Go away, this is for genuine Finns only!" Then I started to sing Marita in Finnish, belting out a sentimental climax on my knees. The arena exploded in a rare joyful bout of laughter, and there I truly felt that despite my diverse background, I had become more of a Finn. I had shown that I understood Finnish Tango and used this understanding to combine cultures in a way that was perceived to be authentic.

5.3 In ourselves we trust

The third element of being yourself is healthy self-confidence. For the purposes of this book self-confidence is defined as the state of mind of a person or a group of persons who believe in their abilities and maintain a constructive attitude towards future outcomes. This belief in your abilities and the maintenance of a positive attitude depends on many of the elements that have been covered in this book. Though we could make a long list of things that have an impact on self-confidence, the main factors to consider are the following:

- Knowledge

- Risk acceptance

- Trust

- Courage

- Experience

- Esteem

The concept of self-confidence is quite appropriately the last of the elements covered in the Possibility Model. The first four factors listed above are all featured in each of the previous four chapters of this book. They culminate here, in forging the foundation of the model's pinnacle: confidence in self. A solid knowledge base is indeed a necessary condition to a heightened state of self-confidence. Too many unknowns make us feel uneasy, and insufficient knowledge sets us up for unnecessary errors that, with time, erode our confidence.

The acceptance of risk and especially of its potentially negative consequences is a critical factor in building self-confidence. To see failure as a natural part of achieving success is quintessential to the notion of sustained self-confidence. The strong belief that, in the end, you will be successful is what often makes the difference between those who achieve and those who don't.

Trust is indicated here as the level of societal trust covered in Chapter 3. This is the trust that we give and receive within a community setting. The fact that I can trust most of my co-citizens and that most of them can trust me forms a synergetic catalyst for everyone's self-confidence.

The fourth element is courage and comes from our discussion of *sisu* in Chapter 4. A good state of self-confidence comes in part from the belief in your ability to go all the way to achieve a desired transformation in your life or in your business. Courage to take a venture to its final destination regardless of the pitfalls and personal trials naturally fuels your level of self-confidence.

Finally, two more elements that have not been directly covered so far are also important in achieving healthy self-confidence. The first of these two is experience. This relates to your previous experiences with success and failure. Levels of self-confidence usually grow with positive experiences of success. You can even express this with a simple formula: self-confidence equals the amount of our successes divided by the number of our failures.

It is important that this equation is considered only as a part of the total state of your self-confidence because successes and failures are necessarily a dynamic set of occurrences that are often out of our direct control. If they were the only source of our self-confidence, it would cause your self-confidence to dangerously fluctuate from over-confidence to insecurity. Though we cannot let our past failures dictate our level of self-confidence, it is undeniable that our past success-to-failure ratio has an impact on our current level of confidence.

To achieve a more stable level of self-confidence, it is thus imperative that we ground it in the other supporting factors listed here. While we accept that failures are often the necessary stepping stones towards success, we must have another set of strong self-confidence anchors to keep our ship from drifting away with the recurrent and inevitable tides of success and failure in our lives.

The last factor on our list is esteem. This refers to both self-esteem and the esteem we receive from others. Esteem and confidence are different concepts that are both at the highest level of Abraham Maslow's hierarchy of needs.[14] They are, according to him, two of the most sophisticated sets of needs in order for humans to achieve self-actualization and ultimately happiness. These are two different and important concepts and thus it is important to distinguish them here.

For many psychologists, esteem is central to a person's psychological health. It comes from the acceptance, love and respect that people direct to themselves and receive from others. Self-esteem is thus the acceptance and respect that one has for oneself.

The definition of healthy self-confidence indicated above is more expansive than the one appearing in many psychology textbooks.

However, most definitions of self-confidence include the notion of belief in the abilities of self. It logically follows that self-esteem can be said to be a pre-condition for self-confidence. The starting point must be to know and accept yourself and your abilities before you can start believing in them.

In Figure 5-4 we have set these six elements of self-confidence in the form of a chain. In the middle of this round chain we indicate the term "value." This refers to anything a person or a company deems to be of value. The self-confidence chain set up in this manner symbolizes one of the important features of healthy self-confidence. It serves as a natural way for people and companies to protect and develop the things they value. When one link of the chain is weakened, the risk of losing something of value increases.

For example, if your self-esteem is low it may well be that it will have a detrimental effect on your relationships with others and the risk of losing or damaging valuable personal relationships will be high. From the corporate perspective, if your company's willingness to take a reasonable amount of

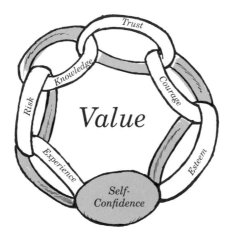

FIGURE 5-4: **The Self-Confidence Chain**

risk is low, the occurrence of successes will also be low. The company's self-confidence chain will be weaker on its link related to risk acceptance and some of the company value will be lost over time.

Finnish self-confidence

If we take the elements of self-confidence indicated above we find that Finnish self-confidence should generally be in good shape. Many of the assets of the Finnish character covered until now naturally fuel a good level of self-confidence for most Finns. The levels of knowledge, social trust and courage as part of *sisu* are at an exceptionally high level in Finland. The vast pool of knowledge available in Finland in a host of disciplines contributes to a high level of national self-confidence. Even in the absence of a specific experience, a high level of acquired knowledge invariably helps people in countries like Finland, with a rich availability of skilled labor to take on endeavors that have never been attempted before.

The high social trust discussed in Chapter 3 is a catalyst for economic success in many countries. It also has a clear and positive impact on the level of confidence of each citizen in these societies. In this context, the degree of trust in the fact that your social group's members will diligently execute a task naturally gives you more confidence in the importance and impact of your own contribution. High trust societies simply allow you to believe that your added contribution will stand on the solid network of supporting contributions of others.

Finally the ability to muster enough courage to face all possible challenges and see a project through all the way to its completion is one of the great boosters of self-confidence. The affinity of most Finns for displaying *sisu* in the wake of performing daunting tasks is a positive part of the national character and a contributing factor in building national and personal self-confidence.

The relationship to error and the acceptance of relative failure, however, is a point that would need improvement in Finland. In fact, many of the distinguished Finns interviewed for this book believed a greater acceptance of failure to be a growth opportunity for most Finns and most Finnish companies. Our discussion of Finnish entrepreneurship as part of the process of trial and error of Chapter 2 supports this view.

The level of your self-confidence is often the mirror image of your attitude towards the potential outcomes of any given venture. If your attitude is accepting of any outcome, good or bad, then your level of self-confidence will increase. When you do not dwell on potentially negative outcomes you worry far less about failure and especially the disapproval of others should failure occur. This attitude allows you to focus more on the actual situation and enhances enjoyment of the process. This ultimately increases the possibilities for success. This is why the definition of self-confidence presented here is not limited to the belief in your abilities but is as much about a positive attitude towards a venture's outcome whatever it may be.

It is interesting that a certain amount of risk averseness exists in some of the best-known proverbs of the Finnish language. One such adage goes: *ken kuuseen kurkottaa, se katajaan kapsahtaa*. The literal translation of this is: "whoever reaches for the tall spruce, falls down onto the juniper." The gist of this woodsy saying is that if you reach for something that is far too good for you, it is not going to end well.

Words of country wisdom like these still support the Finnish culture of relative risk aversion. Though put in the right context they may promote prudence, they can also be taken too literally and seriously cripple initiative. This is especially true if the self-concept of "too good for you" is narrowed by poor self-esteem. Fortunately, attitudes seem to be changing. The levels of ambition are adapting to a global economic landscape that will necessitate greater risk-taking from a larger pool of Finnish workers and entrepreneurs in the future.

As far as self-esteem is concerned, there seems to have been somewhat of a myth created around the perceived poor self-esteem of Finns. In self-esteem researches conducted in Finnish universities, it seems clear that Finns are no different in their level of self-esteem than people from other nationalities.[15] For many foreign observers and a good number of Finns themselves, the belief that Finnish self-esteem was lower than it is elsewhere in the world was perhaps the combination of two things.

First, you can have high self-esteem without verbally communicating this to others. In this regard our discussion of the Finnish culture of silence in Chapter 3 is also relevant here. Many Finns may appear to have lower self-esteem, because of their lower levels of communication. This does not stop them from holding themselves and each other in high esteem. After all, Finland has been determined to be one of the happiest nations on earth. Happiness is, for many psychologists, the measure of a high degree of esteem of self and others.

Second, the difference between self-esteem and self-confidence is not always clear and depends on your interpretation of these terms. What some would point to as being weak self-esteem may actually be a demonstration of weaker self-confidence.

Finally, the impact of experience with success and failure is perhaps another challenge in the Finnish self-confidence equation. This challenge is also related to the relative risk aversion discussed earlier. Certain sets of failures are required as stepping stones for success. If the Finnish psyche resists trials and their necessary errors, this will necessarily affect the number of successes realized. The resulting success-to-failure ratio will produce a lower level of self-confidence over time. If you add to this a culture of silence around failures and even successes, the compound effect might be that Finnish entrepreneurial behavior won't be able to compete with more open and communicative cultures over the long run.

As indicated above, the third driver of being yourself is healthy self-confidence. The word healthy is used as a qualifier here to distinguish the self-confidence described here from the excesses of arrogance or presumptuousness. Arrogance is a state of unhealthy self-confidence because it relies on an unrealistic belief in your abilities. The discrepancy between the real and perceived levels of competence is so large that the risk of engaging in serial failures is high. In addition, this attitude often generates condescending personalities that can rarely attract the sustained trust of others which is critical for generating success.

Presumptuousness is a different form of unhealthy self-confidence, one that does not accept failure as an option. This is a dishonest breed of confidence because success, as we have seen, contains obvious elements of randomness and thus can never be completely assured. This type of overconfidence sets the person or company up for a more damaging fall when failure inevitably occurs. This doubly inhibits further trials because much of the credibility around a person who guarantees success is lost after a single attempt.

Finns are seldom guilty of excesses in self-confidence. As we have seen, the general culture around enterprise is still relatively conservative. There is, however, some appearance of over-confidence in some parts of the self-confidence chain drawn earlier. This is especially true in some of the parts of the chain where Finns usually excel. Because of the high level of Finnish education and professionalism, Finns tend to have a bias for ideas and products made in Finland. This is basically a good thing as long as the discrepancy between reality and presumption is not ridiculously large.

In their recent book on the internationalization of Finnish companies, *Matkanopas*[16], Saku Tuominen and Risto Kuulasmaa interviewed some Finnish opinion leaders on the issue. Of particular interest in the book is a list of challenges typically facing Finnish companies in their forays into international business ventures. One of these challenges is that Finns sometimes have an unrealistic belief in the relative quality of their products. Many of those interviewed corroborated this national myth around Finnish product superiority.

The common belief in Finland has been that if a product doesn't make it internationally it is because of poor Finnish marketing and communication skills. The view expressed here is that this may be a set of misplaced beliefs that are conducive to failure and poor self-confidence in the long term. Realistic belief in yourself and your company should be spread more evenly around the self-confidence chain in order for it to produce better results.

The next two cases are about successful Finns who have developed and exuded a special kind of Finnish self-confidence in their lives and in their businesses.

A lone and confident rider: Hjallis Harkimo

Hjallis Harkimo is one of the most famous figures of the Finnish sports business and one of the country's most successful entrepreneurs. He is also well-known for being the first Finn to have sailed alone around the world in an international sailing competition in 1987. In his opinion, one of the greatest challenges facing Finland for the future is the lack of courage and drive for Finnish companies to take their place in international markets. In his opinion, there are too few Finnish entrepreneurs who have the language skills and the burning desire to grow their businesses into global success stories. He believes that Nokia is the greatest Finnish success story but he is afraid that too few companies will be following in Nokia's footsteps in the future.[17]

In business life, Harkimo is credited with being the driving force behind the construction of the country's largest sports and entertainment facility: the Helsinki Hartwall Arena. His mother Doris is a member of the well-known Hackman family of Finnish industrialists. He has been involved in a host of business ventures in sports marketing, ice-hockey team management, elite athlete management, real-estate development, technology start-ups, etc. He has been the main TV character in Finland's edition of The Apprentice. In some respects, Hjallis Harkimo is Finland's version of Donald Trump.

When asked where he got the self-confidence to achieve his business success, his answer was unequivocal. His several months at sea alone were a defining moment in his life. After that, he believed that he could accomplish anything. The challenge was unique because he was the first Finn to succeed in that venture. It was genuine because of his past as a dyed-in-the-wool sailor. Finally, it warranted a significant amount of belief in his abilities. This huge personal success brought his success-to-failure ratio to a high level and carried his self-confidence over into his life's many successful ventures. Indeed, when you talk about Hjallis Harkimo with the leadership of international ice-hockey, for example, they will all say the same thing: Harkimo is definitely a very strong Finnish personality.

"I'm just a girl from Saarijärvi": Kirsti Paakkanen

In 1945, 16-year-old Kirsti Paakkanen, from the small town of Saarijärvi in central Finland, decided to leave for the big city of Helsinki to attend school. She did this despite her father's initial opposition. On her first night in the war-ravaged city, she called upon some distant relatives as she was looking for a place to stay. Reluctantly, they took her in for just one night. The relatives came back to a house that was completely cleaned, with a warm dinner on the table. The family decided that the young Kirsti Paakkanen could stay. Already then, she was entrepreneurial.

She finished her studies and began working for the international textile sourcing department of the Stockmann department store. She then moved on to work in the advertising industry and decided to establish her own advertising agency in 1969. The agency was called Womena, and it employed only female personnel. It was a risky business and no bank would give her a loan at the outset.

When asked where she found the self-confidence to start her own agency, she remembered a call to her mother asking for advice before taking her first entrepreneurial leap. Her mother simply told her that she was not born to fail. In Kirsti Paakkanen's opinion, mothers should be supportive and communicative in this way to enhance the next generation's confidence in their success.

It turned out to be a very successful business that she ultimately sold to an American conglomerate twenty years later, in 1989. The timing for her was great. Only a couple of years after the sale, Finland would face one of the hardest recessions in its history. At this stage, Kirsti Paakkanen was over 60 years old and had intended to settle into early retirement in Southern France.

In 1991, the famous Finnish textile design house Marimekko, also founded and led by a woman, the iconic Armi Ratia, was on the verge of bankruptcy. As mentioned earlier, Paakkanen decided to come out of retirement and save this institution in distress. She bought the entire company. When her bankers asked her what her objectives were, she answered that she didn't have objectives, she only had a dream. They looked at her with disbelief.

The Amer group, a Finnish tobacco and sporting goods conglomerate, had bought the company in 1985. It had been hemorrhaging losses ever since. The turnaround she pulled off is one of Finland's greatest examples of change management. She transformed the company culture as well as the company's strategy. She put the workers and design specialist at the top of the organizational chart and prioritized quality over quantity. This gave the company its edge back. It is now a listed company on the Finnish stock exchange with a market capitalization of over 100 million Euros.

Paakkanen today lives in Southern France, where she bought the former residence of Norman Foster, the celebrated

English architect. I had the pleasure of visiting her in the house called "la Voile" ("The Sail"), designed by Foster, where she spends a lot of her time with the assistance of a charming French couple. At the age of 82, she still has the wit and charisma she had when she was leading Marimekko. She also exudes the wonderful blend of Finnish healthy self-confidence and humility that often characterizes Finnish success stories. As I left her she held my hands and said: "Please don't be disappointed in me (for this book of yours). I am just a girl from Saarijärvi."

The miracle of you

We have arrived at the end of our journey to the top of the Possibility Model. The stories we have covered have come mostly from Finland and from some exceptional Finns who have made the impossible possible. They have all displayed a notable degree of mastery at some levels of the Possibility Model. They have also illustrated the many different ways you can tackle the sometimes long and perilous climb towards personal and collective success. Their stories are a tribute to the potential of the human spirit and to the way it can be leveraged to generate positive outcomes and, occasionally, something we call a miracle.

The five-level climb we have just completed is a simple metaphor for all those who want to better understand their relative position on the journey towards success. At each one of these levels we have presented a sub-model of three elements that are of critical importance for the successful passage to the next level of possibilities. This charted course has laid down, in this way, 15 conceptual stepping stones that can help elevate us to greater success in the various ventures of our lives.

In Chapter 1, we identified the open mind as a natural starting point for any successful enterprise. We presented a model, the *virtuous circle of the open mind,* which helps keep our minds open and includes knowledge, tolerance and energy. We concluded that Finns enjoy a privileged position at this level because of their high standard of education and their egalitarian social structure.

In Chapter 2, we introduced the *hierarchy of trial and error* in the form of a pyramid with three levels: randomness at the base, cognition in the middle and intuition at the top. We observed the strength of Finns at the level of fact-based cognitive trial and error as well as a relative weakness at the level of intuitive experimentation and risk-taking.

Chapter 3 posited a simple formula to understand the impact of the work we do. The *work utility formula* is the result of effort times the sum of both intelligence and culture. Finland benefits from a high level of work utility with a good work ethic combined with great R&D and a positive culture of trust and social well-being.

Sisu was the theme of Chapter 4. The impact of *sisu* on success was depicted in the image of the *sisu tightrope.* The force of *sisu* is often the power and set of personal features we need to take us from the status quo all the way through to transformation. This potent ingredient in creating possibilities is a combination of courage, tenacity, cool-headedness and even non-compromising stubbornness. It is one of the key features that pulled Finland out of its crises and reinforced its pride as an independent and self-made nation.

Finally, in this fifth chapter, we revealed the three elements of the *Holy Grail of being yourself:* confidence, authenticity and personality. This chapter also introduced new models that attempt to explain the importance of *positive uniqueness* in affirming personality and the workings of the *self-confidence chain* in maintaining our confidence and adding more value to our lives. Finns, like all other people, have a strong set of personal features that make them unique. They are viewed as authentic but need to make sure that all six elements that affect their self-confidence continue to develop.

It has been a long-standing habit of the human condition to pray for a miracle. Perhaps because of this we have been attuned to those who claim or have demonstrated that they can turn water into wine and make the seemingly impossible possible. In the end, our lives are made by what we can generate from within ourselves and what providence may bring our way. Armed with the conceptual tools presented here and potentially inspired by our journey up the Possibility Model, I believe that you are in a better position to succeed in any venture of your choosing and perhaps create, in the same way that Finland and many Finns have done, the *Miracle of You.*

Acknowledgements

The act of writing is a solitary affair. I didn't fully realize the number of long hours and days away from home this creative venture would entail. Despite this relative solitude, there have been many people on the sidelines helping me and wishing me well. I would like to express my thanks here to some of those who have helped me make this book possible. First, I would like to thank my friend Kevin Frazier, who is the kind of erudite editor you can only dream of having on board for a book like this. I would like to thank my boss, Risto Nieminen, for his encouragement and the friendly intellectual challenges he has thrown at me over the years. My colleagues at the Finnish National Lottery have offered me a great backstage view of the daily workings of Finnishness as well as a glimpse at a Finnish Miracle in the making. Thank you for that.

I would also like to thank my friend John Simon for his insights and Mirja Heikkilä for her diligence in assisting me in the demanding research of Finnishness and success. I am also grateful to have found Jan Lindström, an outstanding young graphic designer who seems to be able to make all my impossible ideas look possible. I owe a debt of gratitude to the people at Talentum for having the open-mindedness to support this project. Special thanks go to Katja Hollmén, Heikki Hiltunen, Juha Nurro and Liisa Poikolainen. Being a father of two young children, I sometimes needed a place to stay away from my active family life to write in quieter spaces. My thanks go to my friend Kaija Parjanne and the staff of the House of Writers at Villa-Kivi. This stunning house on Töölö Bay, in the heart of Helsinki, offered a unique setting to write a book about Finnishness. Last, but absolutely not least, I would like to thank my family: my wife Hanna and children Alexandra and Tristan. I look forward to catching up with them on their personal climb towards their dreams.

Appendix 1

I would like to thank the following great Finns for their time in giving their views on Finnishness and success for this book:

- Martti Ahtisaari
- Matti Alahuhta
- Anne Brunila
- Hjallis Harkimo
- Mikael Jungner
- Ilkka Kanerva
- Jukka Karjalainen
- Petri Kokko
- Seppo Kulmala
- Pekka Lundmark
- Raija Mattila
- Risto Nieminen

- Sauli Niinistö
- Kirsti Paakkanen
- Susanna Rahkamo
- Martin Saarikangas
- Kai Seikku
- Risto Siilasmaa
- Timo Soini
- Alexander Stubb
- Harri Syväsalmi
- Anssi Vanjoki
- Peter Vesterbacka
- Lasse Virén

Notes

Chapter 1: An open mind

1 World's Happiest Country Gallup, July 2010. Finland came in second, behind only Denmark as the happiest nation in the world.

2 According to Statistics Finland the industrial output of Finland has increased by over 2200 percent since 1938 (see www.stat.fi/tup/suomi90/toukokuu_en.html). In this regard Finland's economy can be compared to the post-war Japanese economic miracle.

3 See *Women Matter*, an insightful paper on the correlation of corporate success and the role of women, produced by McKinsey & Company in 2007.

4 Veijo Meri, *C.G. Mannerheim, Suomen Marsalkka* (Helsinki: WSOY, 1988), 225–226.

5 "The World's Best Countries," *Newsweek Magazine*, August 2010. A *Newsweek* study of health, education, economy and politics ranked Finland as the best country in the world. See also "The Global Competitiveness Report 2010–2011," World Economic Forum, where Finland came in 7th in the world.

6 Moh Chelali, "The Finnish miracle (English version)," *Teacher News Magazine*, BC Teachers' Federation, volume 23, number 5, March 2011.

7 "How Finland will solve the world's most wicked problems – Consider it solved!" Country Brand Report 25.11.10. Document downloadable at www.tehtavasuomelle.fi.

8 Sirkku Kupiainen, Jarkko Hautamäki and Tommi Karjalainen, *The Finnish education system and PISA* (Helsinki: Ministry of Education Publications, 2009). See also Hannu Simola, "The Finnish Miracle of PISA: historical

and sociological remarks on teaching and teacher education," Comparative Education, vol. 41, No. 4, November 2005, 455–470.

9   The issue of greater freedom in education is taken up in an eloquent and provocative speech of Sir Ken Robinson in his talk in the TED series of lectures (www.ted.com) recorded February 2006 in Monterey, California, USA. In his book *Out of our minds: Learning to be creative* (London, Wiley-Capstone, 2001) he jests about the pressure put upon the very young to perform and to produce CVs with their accomplishments at the tender age of 3. He argues that freedom in education is a driver of success in life and of greater innovation in society.

10 Malcolm Gladwell, *Outliers: The Story of Success* (Camberwell, Vic, Allen Lane, 2008).

11 Richard D. Lewis, *Finland, the Cultural Lone Wolf* (Yarmouth, ME, USA: Intercultural Press, 2005).

12 *The Economist*, "Expats at Work," 14 May 2009.

13 Ben Nothnagel, "Recruiting Top Talent to Create a Globally Competitive Workforce," study presented at VALOA seminar, 18 February 2010.

14 The Times Higher Education World University Rankings 2010–2011 ranks the world's top 200 universities (www.timeshighereducation.co.uk/world-university-rankings/index.html). Only one Finnish university, the University of Helsinki, made it to this list. It ranked 102nd. This same university did a little bit better in the QS 2010 World University Rankings (www.qs.com administered by QS Quacquarelli Symonds Limited) with a global ranking of 75th from a 108th position in 2009. The next best Finnish university is the University of Turku, which is ranked 211th for 2010.

15 The top Finnish venture capital companies have all met difficult times over the past few years. The 3i venture capital firm left Finland a few years ago and manages its Finnish portfolios from Copenhagen and Stockholm. Eqvitec Partners experienced difficulties and sold most of its assets to the Nordic Verdane Capital Advisors. CapMan, a publicly listed company, announced in late 2010 that it shall cease making investments under its technology fund.

16 For a good overview of the European challenges in creating successful start-ups see *Wired Magazine's* issue, "Europe's next billion dollar start-ups," October 2010, 98–108.

17 Author interview with Mikael Jungner on 7 July 2011.

18 These are TEKES, ELY-keskus and at later stages Vera Ventures and SITRA.

19 One measure that the Finnish state could consider is better and more flexible tax incentives for investors and young innovative companies. In France, for instance, new innovative and high-growth potential companies are given a seven year tax break for all R&D expenditures. For private investors, a tax scheme that would allow flexible investment, exit and reinvestment into another promising venture with lower tax liability would also generate much-needed private investment in this area.

Chapter 2: Trial and error

1 William Ross Ashby, *Design for a Brain* (New York: Wiley, 1960).

2 Georges-Hébert Germain, *Céline* (Dundum Press, 1998).

3 Matti Häikiö, *Nokia: The Inside Story* (Pearson Education, 2002).

4 Author interview with Martin Saarikangas, 18 January 2011.

5 Heikki Haapavaara, *Iso-Masa, laivanrakentaja* (Gummerus:Ajatus, Helsinki, 2002).

6 Economics and Statistics Division, WIPO, *World Intellectual Property Indicators* (WIPO Publication 2010).

7 Malcolm Gladwell, *Blink: The Power of Thinking without Thinking* (London: Penguin Books, 2005).

8 Neil Baldwin, *Edison: Inventing the Century* (University of Chicago Press, 2001).

9 Alan Deutschman, *The Second Coming of Steve Jobs* (New York: Broadway, 2001).

10 Author interview with Risto Siilasmaa, 16 June 2011.

11 See a discussion of this point in Pentti Sydänmaanlakka, *Intelligent Leadership: leading people in intelligent organisations* (Espoo: Pertec Consulting), 2007.

12 The Global Entrepreneur Index, 2008.

13 Erkko Autio, "The Finnish Paradox: The Curious Absence of High-Growth Entrepreneurship in Finland" (Helsinki: ETLA, The Research Institute of the Finnish Economy 2009).

14 Statistics of the Finnish Entreprneurship Society (Suomen Yrittäjät) Helsinki, 2011, www.yrittäjä.fi.

15 John Gammack, Valerie Hobbs, Diarmuid Pigott, *The book of informatics* (Australia: South-Western, Cengage Learning Australia, 2006), 368.

16 Mårten Mickos at Aalto University's Centre for Entrepreneurship, "Reaching for the stars," video talk given in October 2009.

17 Author interview with Alexander Stubb on 14 July 2011.

18 Paul Carroll, Chunka Mui, *Billion Dollar Lessons: What You Can Learn from the Most Inexcusable Business Failures of the Last 25 Years* (New York: Portfolio, 2008).

19 Steve Bailey, *Science at the service of physical education and sport* (London: Wileys, 1996). This is a book on the history of the International Council of Sports Science and Physical Education (ICSSPE).

20 This means "We are all heroes" and it is one of the famous songs of J. Karjalainen. Much like Queen's "We are the Champions," it is spontaneously sung by Finns in moments of victory.

Chapter 3: Working harder and smarter

1 On this aspect of Adam Smith, see Jerry Z. Muller, *Adam Smith in His Time and Ours* (New York: Free Press, 1992).

2 Anders K. Ericsson, Michael J. Prietula, Edward T. Cokely, "The Making of an Expert," *Harvard Business Review* (July–August 2007).

3 Malcolm Gladwell, *Outliers: The Story of Success* (Little, Brown and Company, 2008).

4 Tapani Hietaniemi, *Max Weber ja Europan erityistie* [Max Weber and the Distinctive Path of Europe], (Helsinki: Tutkijaliitto,1998); Sven Eliæson & Kari Palonen (eds): Max Weber's Relevance as Political Theorist, Special Issue of Max Weber Studies, 4:2, 2004.

5 Adriano Tilgher, *Work, what it has meant to men through the ages* (Arno Press, 1977) – reprint of 1930 edition.

6 Author interview with Pekka Lundmark on 5 May 2011.

7 John Simon, *Kone's Prince – The Colourful Life of Pekka Herlin* (Helsinki: Otava, 2011).

8 The Kone Corporation is one of Finland's most successful global companies with a turnover of approximately 5 billion Euros in 2010.

9 Sakari Nupponen, "Täällä tehdään hulluna työtä" [Here we work like crazy], *Taloussanomat,* 12 November 2010.

10 According to the OECD's study on the average annual hours actually worked per worker (www.stats.oecd.org) the world's hardest-working nation is Korea with an average annual working time of 2256 hours per worker. The OECD average is 1764 hours per worker. Finland has an average of 1704.

11 See the Global Competiveness Index published by the World Economic Forum in 2010.

12 Matti Nykänen is the most successful ski jumper of all time. He won four gold medals and one silver at the Olympic Games in Sarajevo 1984 and Calgary 1988, as well as a total of 14 World Championship medals between 1982 and 1990.

13 David Halpern, "Trust in Business and trust between citizens," Prime Minister's Strategy Unit, 13 April 2005.

14 Poll published on Gallup.com on 25 October 2007, "Many World Citizens Trust Neighbors More Than Police."

15 Mark J. Ramseyer and Eric B. Rasmusen, "Comparative Litigation Rates," Harvard Law School and Kelly School of Business, 2 December 2010. For the number of Finnish litigation lawyers see The Finnish Bar Association web site: www.asianajajat.fi).

16 See the Transparency International CPI results at www.transparency.org/policy_research/surveys_indices/cpi/2010.

17 Francis Fukuyama, *Trust: The Social Virtues and the Creation of Prosperity* (New York: Free Press, 1995).

18 Aaro Harju, "The Scope of Present Day Civil Society," www.kansalais yhteiskunta.fi.

19 Richard D. Lewis, *Finland, The Cultural Lone Wolf* (London: Intercultural Press, 2005).

20 Peter Drucker, "What Makes an Effective Executive," Harvard Business Review, June 2004.

21 Stephen M. R. Covey, *The Speed of Trust"* (New York, Free Press, 2008), 210.

22 The ELISE report of the European Lotteries Association 2010.

23 Metropolin Hyvinvointi [Well-being in the Metropolitan Area], Helsinki 2010.

24 Manuel Castells, Pekka Himanen, *The Information Society and the Welfare State: The Finnish Model* (New York: Oxford University Press, 2002).

25 Martti Häikiö, *Nokia, Matka maailman huipulle* (Helsinki: Edita, 2009).

26 Author interview with Anssi Vanjoki on 20 April 2011.

27 Martti Häikiö, *Nokia, Matka maailman huipulle* (Helsinki: Edita 2009), 101.

28 André Chaker, Nicolas Arsenault, *Strategies in Mobile Marketing* (London: Baskerville 2002).

29 Saku Tuominen, Risto Kuulasmaa, *Matkanopas [Travel Guide]* (Helsinki: Tammi, 2011).

Chapter 4: Sisu

1   Hudson Strode, "Sisu: A word that explains Finland," *New York Times*, 14 January 1940.

2   Veijo Meri, *Suomen Marsalkka C. G. Mannerheim* (Helsinki: WSOY, 1990), 76.

3   Friends of Finland, "Finland Fights!" Emerson Yorke Studio, New York City, 1939.

4   See Wikipedia – List of casualties during the Second World War and Runo Pääkkönen, "Finns who died, were injured or handicapped in the war," Finnish Institute of Occupational Health, *30 August.*

5   J.E.O. Screen, *Mannerheim: The Finnish Years* (London: Hurst & Co Ltd, 2001).

6   Ben Nothnagel, "Recruiting Top Talent to Create a Globally Competitive Workforce," Presentation at Valoa Seminar 18 February 2010, www.benna.fi.

7   Marjatta Jabe, Helena Häkkinen, *Uljas uusi johtaminen* [*Brave New Leadership*] (Helsinki: Talentum 2010), 265.

8   Eero Kostmo, *Suomalainen johtajuus: Rohkeus olla omintakeinen* [*Finnish Leadership: The Courage to be Original*] (Helsinki: Talentum 2004), 152.

9   Author interview with Timo Soini on 28 June 2011.

10 See National Agency of Health statistics at www.stakes.fi/tilastot.

11 Esa Österberg, *Alkoholin kulutuksen kasvu vuonna 2004* [*Increase in alcohol consumption in 2004*], Tammi 2005.

12 Hannu Niemi, "Rikollisuustilanne Suomessa [Crime Situation in Finland]" II.B.3. Oikeuspoliittinen tutkimuslaitos [National Research Institute of Legal Policy] 2005.

13 Author interview with Harri Syväsalmi, 28 June 2011.

Chapter 5: Being Yourself

1   See TED Talks, "Ben Saunders skis to the North Pole," filmed in February 2005, www.ted.com.

2   Chris Anderson, *The Long Tail: Why the Future of Business Is Selling Less of More* (New York: Hyperion, 2006).

3   Joseph B. Pine, Kim C. Korn, *Infinite Possibility: Creating Customer Value on the Digital Frontier* (San Francisco: Berrett-Koehler Publishers, 2011).

4   Author interview with Susanna Rahkamo and Petri Kokko on 19 July 2011.

5 Author interview with Sauli Niinistö on 19 July 2011.

6 RISC Monitor, "Minäkeskeisyyden kasvu huolettaa suomalaisia [The growth of self-centeredness worries Finns," June 2011. This research conducted by TNS Gallup reveals that individualistic values in Finland are rising, such as hedonism, differentiation and sex-identity.

7 Mission for Finland, Country Brand Report, 25 November 2010.

8 Author interview with Martti Ahtisaari on 19 May 2011.

9 Interview with Peter Vesterbacka on 29 June 2011.

10 James H. Gilmore, B. Joseph Pine, *Authenticity: What Consumers Really Want* (Boston: Harvard Business School Press, 2007).

11 Gilmore & Pine, *Authenticity*, 95.

12 Jutta Jaakkola,"The Finnish Tango: Its History and Characteristics," *Finnish Music Information Service*, trans. Susan Sinisalo, May 2000.

13 Author interview with Jukka Karjalainen on 26 June 2011.

14 Abraham H. Maslow, *Toward a Psychology of Being* (London: Wiley, 3rd Edition, 1998).

15 Katariina Salmela-Aro, Jari-Erik Nurmi, *"Self-esteem during university studies predicts career characteristics 10 years later,"* Journal of Vocational Behavior magazine, 2007.

16 Saku Tuominen, Risto Kuulasmaa, *Matkanopas* [*Travel Guide*] (Helsinki, Tammi 2011), 148.

17 Author interview with Hjallis Harkimo, 27 June 2011.

Index

Abloy; 71

Agostini Giagomo; 129

Agricola Mikael; 114

Ahtisaari Martti; 214–217

Alahuhta Matti; 135

Aldrin Edwin; 201

Amer Corporation; 77, 246

Andersson Chris; 209

Angélil René; 67–68

Apple; 56, 72, 74, 150, 153

Arduin Dominick; 179–180, 200–201

Armstrong Neil; 201

Ashby W Ross; 65

Auraviihde Oy; 233

Autio Erkko; 81

Barack Obama; 199

Beatles; 109

Beckham David; 123

Béliveau Jean; 226

Bezos Jeff; 75

Biotie; 124

Boklöv Jan; 127

Calvin Jean; 113

Carnival Cruises; 69

Clinton Bill; 215

Cousteau Jacques; 231

Covey Stephen M. R.; 139

Crisis Management Initiative (CMI); 215

Cygnaeus Uno; 44

da Silva Ferrera; 100–101

Data Fellows; 76–77, 149

De Melo Augusto; 101

Degerman Patrick; 200

Diack Lamine; 102–103

Digital Chocolate; 219

Dikert Kim; 219

Dion Céline; 35–36, 67

Dion Michel; 67

Disney; 74, 220

Drucker Peter; 138

EA; 220

Edison Thomas; 73–74

Einstein Albert; 19
Elcoteq; 71
Electronic Arts; 219
Elop Stehpen; 135
Enpocket; 156
Ericsson; 68, 108, 147–148
Ericsson Anders; 103
Exxon; 75
Facebook; 150, 152, 218, 222
Fiskars; 125
Fogelholm Gustaf; 145
Fosbury Dick; 126–127
Foster Norman; 246–247
F-Secure; 75, 77, 149
Fukuyama Francis; 134–136
Gates Bill; 75, 109–110, 162
General Electric; 74
Gilmore James; 223–224
Gladwell Malcolm; 49, 73, 109
Google; 56, 150, 153–154, 218
Granit Ragnar; 123
Granlund Mikael; 131
Grönholm Marcus; 118
Gustafsson Veikka; 200
Habeler Peter; 200
Haider Jörg; 184
Hakulinen Veikko; 177
Halonen Tarja; 37, 42–43
Halpern David; 132
Hannula Antti; 76
Harju Arsi; 101
Harkimo Doris; 224
Harkimo Hjallis; 224–225
Hautamäki Antti; 142

Hed Mikael; 219
Hed Niklas; 219
Herlin Antti; 135
Herlin Pekka; 116
Hermes; 223
Hewlett-Packard; 219
Himanen Pekka; 143
Hitler Adolf; 169–170
Holkeri Harri; 98, 101
Hoover Herbert; 167
Hyppönen Ari; 76
Häggman Bjarne; 97
Häggman Pirjo; 93, 96–97
Häkkinen Mika; 118
IBM; 74, 150, 153
Idestam Fredrik; 144–146
Iisalo Jaakko; 219
Iittala; 125
Ilkka Tapani; 101
Immonen Riitta; 77
IObox; 78, 83
Isometsä Jari; 194
Jobs Steve; 74–75, 220
Jungner Mikael; 61
Kairamo Kari; 148, 182
Kalevala Koru; 229
Kanerva Ilkka; 97–98, 101–102
Kankkunen Juha; 118
Kari Tapio; 113
Karjalainen Jukka; 234
Katainen; 55
Kaurismäki Aki; 151–152
Kekkonen Urho Kaleva; 22,
    24–26, 185

Kinnunen Laila; 233
Kirvesniemi Harri; 177, 194
Kirvesniemi Marja-Liisa; 89, 177
K-mart; 223
Koivu Jukka; 225
Koivu Mikko; 225
Koivu Saku; 225–228
Kokko Petri; 211
Kokkonen Ere; 95
Kolehmainen Hannes; 87
Komi Paavo; 90–91, 126
Kone; 71, 116, 125, 135
Konecranes; 115, 125
Koriseva Arja; 233
Kostamo Eero; 183
Kulmala Seppo; 233
Kuulasmaa Risto; 153
Lao Tzu; 205
Le Pen Jean-Marie; 184
Ledwidge Bernard; 52
Lemieux Mario; 226
Leskinen Väinö; 155
Lewis Carl; 87
Lewis Richard D. 137
Lindén Suvi; 102
Linna Väinö; 171
Lipponen Paavo; 55
Lordi; 34–37
Lundmark Pekka; 115
Luther Martti; 105, 113–114, 186
Madonna; 64
Makkonen Matti; 72
Mannerheim C. G. E.; 32,
    163–170, 173–1745

Mannerheim Sophie; 32
Marimekko; 77–78, 223, 229,
    246–247
Markkula Mike; 74
Marvel; 221
Marx Karl; 112
Masa-Yards; 69, 91
Maslow Abraham; 238
Matikainen-Kallström Marjo;
    177–178
Mattila Karita; 117
McCartney Paul; 110
Medvedev Dmitri; 220
Merikanto Oskar; 33, 117
Messier Mark; 226
Mickos Mårten; 84–84
Microsoft; 72, 74–75, 150, 153
Mieto Juha; 89, 177
Milosevic Slobodan; 215
Mobicus; 155–156
Motorola; 86
Mozart Wolfgang Amadeus; 64
Myllylä Mika; 194–195
MySQL; 83–84
Mäkinen Tommi; 118
Mälkki Susanna; 117
Nieminen Toni; 127
Nokia; 13, 56, 68–69, 71–72,
    75, 77, 81, 116, 135, 138,
    144–151, 153–154, 156, 177,
    182, 221, 229, 244
Nokia Tyres; 229–231
Nortel; 151
Nothnagel Ben; 181

Nurmi Paavo; 87, 89, 117, 127, 160, 167, 177
Nykänen Matti; 127
O'Brien Conan; 42
Obama Barack; 199
Ollila Jorma; 138, 149
Orava Sakari; 123
Osho Rajneesh; 9
Ovaskainen Jari; 78, 83
Paakkanen Kirsti; 77–78, 245–246
Panula Jorma; 117
Parvela Timo; 42
Pasolini Renzo; 129
Pihlakoski Antti; 97, 102
Piirainen Jari; 93
Pine Joseph; 209, 223
Polón Eduard; 145–146
Ponsse; 71
Pound Richard; 194
Putaansuu Tomi; 35
Rahkamo Susanna; 211–212
Ratia Armi; 77, 246
Relander Kaj-Erik; 86
Remedy Entertainment; 218
Reno Ginette; 67
RitolaVille; 87
Roberts Kenny; 129
Rosberg Keke; 118
Rousseau Jean-Jacque; 222
Rovio; 75, 151, 218–221
Rung Marion; 36
Rushdie Salman; 220
Ryti Risto; 24, 168

Räikkönen Kimi; 118, 207
Saariaho Kaija; 117
Saarikangas Martin; 69, 91–92, 94–97, 152
Saarinen Jarno; 128–130
Salminen Matti; 117
Salonen Esa-Pekka; 117
Salora-Luxor; 148
Samaranch Juan Antonio; 90, 96
Samsung; 150
Santa Claus; 16, 192
Saraste Jukka-Pekka; 117
Sartre Jean-Paul; 222
Saunders Ben; 201
Sibelius Jean; 33, 117, 160, 167
Siemens; 147
Siilasmaa Risto; 75–77, 149
Smart Paul; 129
Smith Adam; 108
Soini Timo; 184–186
Soininen Hilkka; 123
Sonera; 56, 86
Sony BMG; 36, 233
Sorainen Anna; 96
Sotomayor Javier; 127
Stalin Joseph; 166, 169
Stubb Alexander; 85, 206
Sulake; 218
Syväsalmi Harri; 194–195
Taavitsainen Marita; 234–235
Tallberg Peter; 101
Telefonica; 78
Tikkanen Henrik; 119

Tocqueville Alexis; de 136
Torvalds Linus; 30, 117
Toyota; 154
Trulli Jarno; 130
Trump Donald; 244
Tuominen Saku; 153, 243
Turunen Tarja; 34
Vanjoki Anssi; 144, 148
Vanni Mikko; 102
Vatanen Ari; 118
Weber Max; 112
Vennamo Veikko; 185
Vesterbacka Peter; 219–221
Westerlund Björn; 147
Westermarck Jukka; 123
Wikström Arvid; 146

Wilde Oscar; 204
Virén Lasse; 102–103, 178–179
Virolainen Juho-Pekka; 155
Virta Olavi; 233
Virtanen Artturi Ilmari; 122
Voelter Heinrich; 144–145
Vohlonen Tuomas; 122
Womena; 245
Woods Tiger; 118
Wozniak Steve; 74
Vuitton Louis; 223
Vuorinen Juha; 191
Väkeväinen; Jarno 219
Wärtsilä; 69, 116, 125
Yeltsin Boris; 215
Zynga; 219